think black

An Introduction to Black Political Power

Frank McQuilkin

Consulting Editor
Nathan Hare, Ph.D.
Founder, Black Studies Institute
San Francisco State College
Publisher, *The Black Scholar*

Introduction
Yosef ben-Jochannan, Ph.D.
Chairman, African and African-American
Studies Department
Harlem Preparatory School

The Bruce Publishing Company/New York

Dedicated to the memory of

Langston Hughes

a very black poet

Library of Congress Catalog Card Number: 75-132465

THE BRUCE PUBLISHING COMPANY, NEW YORK
COLLIER-MACMILLAN CANADA, LTD., TORONTO, ONTARIO

Made in the United States of America

contents

introduction

In evaluating the struggles and contributions made by the African-Americans in the United States of America, most historians and other social science writers often overlook those individuals and organizations that preceded the era of their own personal involvement. Thus it was common in the early 1900s for Dr. William E. B. DuBois and his Niagra Movement (which in 1909 became the National Association for the Advancement of Colored People—NAACP) to condemn the works of Booker T. Washington and his associates at Tuskegee Institute in the late 1800s. By the same token Marcus Mosiah Garvey and his Universal Negro Improvement Association (UNIA) constantly attacked Dr. DuBois and the NAACP for their integration stance in the 1920s; the NAACP in turn counterattacked the "back to Africa" separatist stance of the UNIA and Garvey. Today many of the disciples of the late Malcolm X (al hajji Malik Shabazz) and the late Rev. Dr. Martin Luther King, Jr. equally tend to belittle the contributions made by Garvey and the UNIA. Yet they wear the red, black and green buttons and fly flags of the same colors which are commonly known as the African Nationalist colors —introduced and popularized by the UNIA and its founder, Garvey. Even Malcolm X and Dr. King are to an extent becoming names of the past to many of the younger African-Americans whose outlook seems to be destined toward the so-called "Third World" or "New Left." Because of this traditional behavior pattern of the young with regard to their elders, this work may appear to have ignored: (a) the struggle for industrial education for the blacks led by Booker T. Washington's forces in the 1800s; (b) the fight for political equality for the blacks before the Bar of Justice in the federal courts spearheaded by the NAACP from the 1900s to the present; (c) the reawakening of the blacks to their African identity and heritage, and the push for the development of black-owned businesses championed by the UNIA and other African nationalist movements on the street corners of the U.S. until now when young blacks of the late 1960s have caught on to the "Black is Beautiful" cultural revolution currently in progress. Yet when one reflects upon the fact that this young African-American author is primarily addressing young European-Americans about what black peoples are saying and doing, the impression of his ignoring the contributions of certain past and present Negro leaders and their organizations is quickly laid to rest. On the other hand, no one who has followed black America's struggle for human rights could seriously dispute that, in the black-white confrontation, each successive decade regards many of the black revolutionaries of the preceding decade as "Uncle Toms" or "Aunt Tomasinas." Actually, most of those who were called revolutionaries in the past were no more "Toms" or "Tomasinas" than the current black leaders are "militants"; for in either case, it is the same individuals within the so-called "white power structure" that label each group with these terminologies—including "responsibles" or "irresponsibles." The author has carefully avoided these types of name-calling, charges, and counter-charges against individuals and organizations by dealing with the current "social revolution" of the African-Americans (blacks) from the point of their positive contributions rather than the projection of a negative analysis. As such he has been able to speak to young white America in an academic manner rarely achieved by most writers on the subject of what young black America is saying, demanding, and doing; where they are finding most of their frustrations, and where they are going.

One may tend to cite the achievements of the non-violent movements of the civil rights struggle during the late 1950s and 1960s (led by the NAACP, the National Urban League (NUL), the Congress of Racial Equality (CORE), and the Southern Christian Leadership Conference (SCLC) founded by the late Rev. Dr. Martin Luther King, Jr.) in order to counteract the indictment made by this author. But to try and equate the *integrationist* movement with the current *separatist* movement is like trying to turn a butterfly back into a worm. For it is obvious that most of the young leaders of the current black power and other separatist movements were former adherents of the above listed non-violent movements. And because of their frustrations in such movements they found it necessary to form their own organizations, with their own goals, and in most instances financed by themselves. In the case of the young black people, whose views this author shares, it is obvious from the depth of their own indictment that, before adopting the in-between course they now seem to pursue, they had also examined and evaluated the early struggles between the NAACP under W.E.B. Dubois and the UNIA headed by Marcus M. Garvey, as well as the quality of leadership provided by the late James Weldon Johnson (creator of the "Negro national anthem"—"Lift Every Voice and Sing"), Walter White, and, currently, Roy Wilkins. At the same time, they have decided that the civil rights non-violent movements are run by men whose average ages are at least fifty. And these men cannot visualize why the young blacks cannot understand the integrationist and amalgamationist stance of an era now gone by. In this work, the young black separatists are saying to the older integrationist organizations and their "Negro leadership": "You have done very well in your time, but the little you have achieved in more than one hundred years in social integration is now offset by the present drive for economic prosperity and black pride in black communities; and because you are still programmed towards the 'black and white unite' creed of the late 1930s, we must separate from your negroism, for Black is Beautiful." It is therefore not a question of right or wrong, but of *time* and *solution.*

No one in his right mind, including the young blacks in the "New Left," the "Black Nationalist Movement," the "Third World," the "African Nationalist Movement," the "Black Muslims," or the "Five Percenter Movement," can ignore the legal successes of the NAACP during the era of the Scottsboro trial and other major cases wherein young blacks were being railroaded and lynched with city, state, and federal government sanctions. Nor can they ignore the successes of the National Urban League and its local state branches in placing qualified young blacks into white collar jobs in private industry and government. And this young black author has not overlooked these things. He has accepted even Dr. Martin Luther King, Jr.'s "sit-ins," "sleep-ins," and the grand "March on Washington, D.C."; but he is also saying that the young blacks appreciate that those goals are now passé, and achieve very little in terms of the current struggles for black ownership of the economic life of black communities throughout America. He points to the ethnic communities of America, white and non-white, for support of his statement, and in almost every case it is proven that communities are controlled and dominated by one dominant ethnic group in terms of sheer numerical figures except those of blacks.

Throughout history mankind seems to have referred to the generation gap that we too speak about, but in reality it is the generation challenge. For instance, the old diehards in the current civil rights movements are entrenched professionals whose entire lives have been spent trying to attain their dream of a united, "multi-colored," integrated America—and, incidentally, whose activities in this connection provide their livelihoods. They oppose the separatist policies of today's adventurous young black leaders who cannot relive the past of their parents, who cannot follow the same trails, and who cannot apply to present problems the same solutions used in the early and middle 1960's. Unfortunately, the integrationist leaders within the civil rights movements have come to believe in their cause ritualistically, whereas the young blacks see the basics of said *ritualism* at the point when it is at its ebbtide. The irony of it all is that the civil righters and integrationists were just a few short years ago considered the "irresponsible radicals" of their generation and suffered the same ostracism by "white liberals" and their "Negro leaders" of previous years.

"Is there a middle ground to all of this?" those who fear the rocking of the boat always ask. Sadly enough the middlers are the silent ones who wait to gather the spoils of war—the spoils being the end result of the head-on clash and ultimate liquidation of the two groups of fighting blacks—Negroes versus African-Americans—both of whom must ultimately suffer.

In Chapter One, the author attempts to recapture an element in the black American heritage which the civil righters of the past had so wantonly ignored in order to gain a measured sense of acceptance by their white Anglo-Saxon models. This, of course, is not said to demean in any way the dedicated people leading the movements. It does, however, spell out a basic fallacy in the movements. The author has reversed all

8

of this; things African are re-appraised and even carried back to the Garvey days of the UNIA's "back to Africa" movement. Yet there is an element of the "old leftism" led by Dr. W.E.B. DuBois (a violent opponent of Garvey) and the "white liberals" of the early 1930s NAACP era, but this is overshadowed by the "new leftism" once seen in the early days before the Black Panthers also became integrated under the banner of "black and white unite." Of course it is only natural that the young blacks would have adopted many of the world's revolutionaries as symbolic leaders, if only because they are fighting the same person or country considered *the enemy.* In this case, the enemy is the United States and all others who support what young people have come to realize as "imperialism." This does not mean that the blacks, revolutionaries if you will, would accept a country in which they are a majority ruled by any other group than themselves; and this is the cardinal point being overlooked by their critics who can see no good whatsoever in "black activism" as they once saw no good in "Negro-white unionism" —at the time called "black and white unite."

What basically seems to excite and bother most people, both black and white, connected with the civil rights movements of the past and present about young black writers of this kind? They fear them as the reincarnation of Garveyism. They see them as the "tiger cubs" Garvey boasted would follow him when someone jokingly said that he was a "caged tiger" during his incarceration by federal marshalls before his controversial trial and conviction for allegedly "using the U.S. Mail to defraud." But, more so they are afraid of these young black nationalists because they have begun to utter the same "back to Africa" slogans Garvey uttered as he rallied millions of African-Americans to his cause from 1917 to 1925. In turn these young blacks see the civil righters as the obstruction on their way to victory.

In retrospect, the author uses Chapter One to highlight certain aspects of basic biblical truths connected with Africa's history which are generally not seen as such. He writes of Abraham's birth in order to show that Africa's greatness even predated the birth of the father of the Hebrew people and the beginning of the traditional story of the Garden of Eden in the Book of Genesis (the first book of the Old Testament). Although not in great detail, this chapter touches upon the great empires of West Africa from the period of about A.D. 300 to 1591 before the arrival of the first white men (the Portuguese) in West Africa for trade, and not as the standard bearers of Christianity as they once had paid their missionaries to pronounce. Using Africa, the ancestral homeland of the African-Americans or black people, to show how far into antiquity their heritage of greatness extends, the author also touches very briefly on the greatest of the noted West African empires—Ghana (A.D. 300–1076), Mali (A.D. 1238–1488), and Songhay (A.D. 1488–1591). Of course the author could have carried us into greater depths of religious history in which the Africans and their continent played major biblical roles—Moses (an African) fleeing the armies of another African—the Pharaoh, Ramses II—in the Passover drama; also the presentation of the Ten Commandments to Moses on Mount Sinai—all ten, plus the other one hundred and thirty-seven already in use by fellow Africans of Egypt before Moses was born, known as the "Negative Confessions."

Unfortunately, this work cannot deal in any greater detail with the subject matter of Chapter One, which many people would of necessity require volumes of chronological documentation to prove that which the author has so far adequately revealed. However, the brief treatment does open to young investigators and students of "black studies" the possibility of deeper research into the facts so far stated. The author shows that the correspondence between the King of Mani-Congo and his counterpart in Portugal indicated the equality with which each held the other as monarchs, and not as "black" or "white" contestants. The treatment of the rapid disintegration of the commercial and political relationship that existed between the West Africans and West Europeans from the days of Prince Henry (the so-called "Navigator") around A.D. 1444 to the early 1500s is added as support by the author of the facts showing that the Africans had developed major trading centers causing the envy of European traders, pirates, and exploring colonizers until the early nineteenth century when they came to Africa. And this remained true until the European powers were forced finally to let loose the Gold Coast (presently called the Republic of Ghana) in 1957 because of the leadership of its nationalist leader and liberator, Dr. Kwame Nkrumah.

Using Langston Hughes's poem "The Negro Speaks of Rivers" (as he has used others at the beginning and end of most chapters), the author tactfully moves his readers from the ancient African past and brings them into the present, yet reminding them of the fact that it is folly to project the view that black America had no valid past.

The author stabs at the general mythology which African-Americans have had to fight against as much as they have had to struggle for existence itself. He speaks of the myths that originated in the minds of the ignorant European-American (white) masses because of their need to compensate for their own unfortunate economic plight—ignorance planted by their fellow historians, anthropologists, sociologists, and others, each knowing too well his or her disservice to truth, and the racist climate they were creating (the fruits of which today's generations are reaping). He delves deeply into the self-destructive past of the African-Americans, caused by continued brainwashing of their African forebears brought to the Americas and the Caribbean Islands to slave for their European and European-American self-appointed masters; showing how European traditions were glorified and carried forward while those of the Africans were maligned, denied, and even stomped out. He lays down in Chapter Two what might be considered the crux of the following contemporary dissertation, especially the message under the subtitle, "Rejecting a Homeland." Herein also lie the root-causes of the American dilemma (so aptly described by the Swedish author Gunnar Myrdal in his timely book of the same name dealing with the cancerous racist structure of American society) pointed out so succinctly by this young African-American in this, his first work. Also under this subtitle, the bill of particulars for the indictment which follows in Chapter Three and throughout the book has been clearly defined.

In Chapter Three, the author more or less destroys the myth of an "American dream" for all Americans, citing that in reality it is only for various shades of white Europeans and European-Americans—even those having African blood in their veins (ancestry). He therefore begins laying the foundation necessary to show the Africans' and finally the African-Americans' involvement in building the United States into whatever it is today. That without the fruits of the Africans' and their descendants' labor this could not have been realized. And that while in their bondage, they had nevertheless produced to the ultimate degree of their capacity as professionals, semi-skilled and skilled workers, because of the knowledge they brought from Africa by way of the Caribbean Islands.

The author's clarity of understanding in his projection of the "bonded servant" role of both blacks and whites, followed by the freedom of the whites from this bondage, while the blacks were held in perpetual slavery, opens to the average American an area of historical interpretation seldom projected when dealing with the reasons behind what is today called "crime in the streets"—the new passwords for "stop the niggers." And as he continues on through the pages of the chapter, the author has been able to see some parallels in Nazi Germany's persecution and extermination of the Jews with that of the genocide perpetrated by the European colonialists and early independent European-Americans against the red and black men, women, and children of America.

Chapters Four through Sixteen highlight the charges in the author's indictment. At times he calls upon historical bits of information in citing specifics, such as the struggles by Frederick Douglass against his slave "master," and then against white American society in general.

To comment further on this work, which I believe to be timely and descriptive of the current aspirations and feelings of young black America and many of their elders who are flexible enough to see beyond their personal economic security, will in no meaningful way add to its greatness. This book speaks clearly, loudly, and authoritatively.

Yosef ben-Jochannan, Ph.D.
Chairman, African and African-American Studies Department
Harlem Preparatory School

africa: a bright continent

1

Africa has been called the "dark continent." And in this context dark doesn't mean beautiful, but *unknown, mysterious,* and *threatening.* Significantly, Africa has been called dark only by people *outside* Africa. And this seems to be this great continent's biggest difficulty: to be misunderstood by outsiders. Who are these outsiders? Mostly Europeans, and even Americans of the past several hundred years. They neither knew the history of Africa, nor recognized the marvelous talents of Africans. They put labels on Africa and its citizens, they labeled the continent dark, and its citizens primitives, natives, or even savages.

If Africa is dark, it is only so because of the label put on it by people who do not know it. In reality, this continent and its people have given to the modern world much light concerning man's history; they have made great contributions in the areas of art—especially sculpture—music, literature, religion, mineral wealth, and industrial achievement. In return for these gifts, Africans have received little appreciation and much misunderstanding. The record should be set straight. Men and women of today should bring Africa out of the "darkness" of their own minds, and place it in its full, honest light. The rewards for doing so are great, and well worth the effort.

A Long, Long History

In a real sense, all men today owe a personal debt to the African continent, because scientists today seem in agreement that Africa was the birthplace of mankind. Man's cradle seems to have been in the south-eastern part of the land surrounding Lake Tanganyika.[1]

   With the passage of the centuries, and the distribution of man throughout Africa, great civilizations arose. We are familiar with the most famous of these, of course—Egypt. But this foremost African kingdom was itself the result of a widespread north African culture that extended all across the upper part of the continent. It began around 4100 B.C., with the introduction of the world's first solar system; and scientists believe that at that time the Sahara was not a desert, but a kind of vast prairie filled with life. When we consider that the Great Pyramid at Gizeh was built around eight hundred years before the birth of Abraham,[2] father of the Jewish people, we get some idea of how far back into history the greatness of African civilization extends. Europe at that time had nothing which could remotely compete with the accomplishments of Africa.

   But there were other great states in Africa that followed, ones we have never heard about because of some faulty conceptions about history which we will discuss later. The Kingdom of Kush (Cush), for example, began over a century before the birth of Jesus Christ and flourished for at least five hundred years. After its downfall, the kingdom of Ethiopia, predecessor of modern Ethiopia, took over the leadership. Ethiopia, incidentally, became the first nation to adopt Christianity as its national religion.[3] In the seventh century, the followers of Mohammad took control of northern

Africa,[4] and established a civilization that was eagerly imitated by much of Europe. West Africa was marked by a succession of various empires: Ghana, Mali, Songhay, Ashante, Benin, the Haura States, and others, all of which established order, civilization, and trade.[5] Throughout the Middle Ages trade with Europe flourished. In fact, gold from Africa became an important part of European economy. On the eastern coast of Africa trade routes extended as far as Indonesia and China.[6]

Historical evidence only now being uncovered and made known completely contradicts the lie made popular by nineteenth-century historians, and which continues even today: that Africa was a "dark continent," populated by savages half ape, half man, swinging from the trees. The greatest lie of all, of course, is that Africans had to await the arrival of Europeans, the "great white hunters," to be "civilized." Africans enjoyed the benefits of their own civilization centuries before outsiders decided to slice up the continent[7] and declare its people "uncivilized."

Our culture has given us many misconceptions. When we think of Africa, we seldom think in terms of a truly great society: we think of savages in jungles, leading correspondingly savage lives. The faulty histories of the past have given us this idea, and this false impression has passed over into popular American folklore. The fact is, if we are to think *truth,* we must change our attitude towards Africa and towards its history.

Despite the difficulties of climate in some areas, of land-cultivation, and of untamed diseases, the African people managed to meet this often harsh environment, overcome it, and successfully build effective social groupings. This triumph of the African people constitutes one of the great adventure stories of history, and one which fills an important chapter in man's on-going domination over the earth. The history of mankind would surely be far poorer without it.

Europe: A Bad Neighbor

Even though the Sahara trails presented a great challenge, and the western sea routes were largely unexplored, Africa carried on successful commerce with Europe for centuries.[8] This long period of relative mutual benefit came to an end, however, in the 1500s, with the introduction of gunpowder and rifles. During this period, also, we see the opening up of sea routes around the entire coast of Africa by Europeans.[9] Now up to this time, age-old traditions dominated Africa: the local chief, regional king, or emperors ruled by virtue of age, wisdom, the respect of the community, and, if necessary, force. In the 1500s, however, especially on the west coast of Africa, Europeans introduced rifles and gunpowder, for purposes of trade and of domination. Now, for the first time in modern history, Europe became actually stronger than Africa. Chiefs and kings were no longer secure on their thrones without guns and the force that these implied.

So, we see at the time the beginning efforts made to secure guns; with the passage of time, this effort would reach huge proportions. No price became too great to pay for the precious commodity; even human beings were sold for guns. Thus began the establishment of the modern world's sale of men—slaves—between Africa and Europe, and, later on, with the New World. Contemporary mankind still pays the price of his forefathers, who made force more important than human values.

Even in the early 1500s, Europe's relationship to Africa had deteriorated greatly. Nizinga Mbemba, King of Mani-Congo,[10] complained in one of his many letters to the King of Portugal about the conduct of the Portuguese: "we cannot reckon how great the damage is. . . . and so great, Sire, is the corruption and licentiousness, that our country is being depopulated."[11] Unfortunately, such complaints were not listened to, and Europe became not merely a bad neighbor, but a destructive one.

Africa has been compared to a large pie which Europe decided to slice up for herself. Everyone wanted a "slice" of Africa as a sort of status symbol. One after another, the nations came to claim the African people's land as their own territory; the African nations thus became "colonies," the African people became "natives." The Portuguese, the English, the French, the Dutch, the Germans, the Belgians, the Italians, the Spaniards —all of them—turned a proud people with a long history into dependent colonies and despised natives. Africa was no longer ruled by Africans, and her people— the men and woman who had overcome enormous difficulties to build great cultures—were looked upon as savages in a dark continent.

We have been given a rather one-sided view of history—a European one. Think, for example, how the adventures of explorers like Vasco de Gama are praised in our history books. In reality, these so-called explorers were men who were not out to discover new knowledge of the earth and its people, but a group of half-pirates who raided, stole, raped, killed, and burned up and down the coasts of Africa wherever their ships happened to land. And frequently this was done even in the name of Christianity. An account of the destruction of Kilwa, on the eastern coast of Africa, relates how the Portuguese came ashore led by priests holding crucifixes; they formed a procession, sang hymns, and prayed. Then the men proceeded to plunder the town of everything valuable. Several days later, they set it on fire.[12] Perhaps then they resumed their interrupted prayer.

It is important to look for meaning behind the myriad facts which historians are finally bringing to light and looking at truthfully. What did this mean that men from one country could go to another's country, claim it for their own, and reduce its people to servant status? What attitude does this give evidence to? We can say, looking back, that western nations have been suffering for centuries from a false superiority complex. The results have neither been happy for the western nations, nor for the other nations in the world. To much of the world, Europe and the United States seem to be neighborhood bullies. And, for some strange reason, these bullies think they are better than others! Evidence for this can be cited. Not only was Africa bullied into submission, but many countries of Asia and South America also were. Frequently these countries had cultures far older and more impressive than anything Europe could show. The simple fact is that Europe was militarily stronger and more aggressive. These, incidentally, are the two traits that make up a bully.

Some will say that Europe was simply superior to Africa; that Africa is, and was, a "backward" country. This is open to challenge. Africa built pyramids when Europe had cave men; the ancient kingdom of Ethiopia was famous even in the time of Jesus Christ. African states rose and declined when Europe was going through the "dark ages." And the Muslim civilization in the medieval period was also imitated all over Europe. Africa is the second largest continent, and surely not all areas were as advanced technologically as others. This was true for Europe also. But we can safely say that living conditions in Africa throughout the Middle Ages were comparable to those in Europe; in fact, they might very well have been better. When we think of facts like the Hundred Years War, the slavery of serfs, the plagues that depopulated Europe, the burning of witches, the religious fanaticism that made one man burn another in the name of God, Africa seems like a vacation resort! At the very least, looking at those centuries, Europe cannot bathe in a comfortable assurance of superiority.

Europe's so-called superiority actually lies in two areas: force and technology. We must grant that in these cases Europe ran far ahead of Africa, Europe became stronger, and developed a highly technical type of civilization. We can ask this question, however, on what basis do we judge a civilization? On its wealth? The height of its buildings? The strength of its army? The number of its bombs? Or perhaps, the happiness established between its people and the land they live on.

Here, we must judge ourselves and the civilization we have built. We have wealth, buildings, armies, and enough bombs to destroy the world. Besides this, we have millions of people emotionally sick, thousands upon thousands who are in mental hospitals, and a land which is being sapped of all its natural resources. We have poisoned our rivers, poisoned our air, and continue to poison our own minds with false ideas about superiority.

We have much to learn from the history of Africans, who evolved societies basically more peaceful, stable, and happier than our own.[13] It would have been interesting to have watched the evolution of this land of Africa if it had been left alone.

The White Man's "Burden"

All people in the world are colored—either red, yellow, white, brown, or black. The white man has declared the non-whites to be backward—that it is his burden to "civilize" them. This is a fable which, unfortunately, men have come to believe. We see this in Africa's case. The destruction begun by Europeans at the beginning of the modern era grew greater and greater. By the last century, the entire continent was in havoc, with its traditional structures falling apart. European countries stepped in to stop the havoc they themselves had begun. *Colonies, natives, dark continent.* This was how Europe regarded long centuries of civilization by a brave and an inventive people. We can ask, who really burdens whom?

"The Negro Speaks of Rivers"

—Langston Hughes

I've known rivers:
I've known rivers ancient as the world and older than the
   flow of human blood in human veins.

My soul has grown deep like the rivers.

I bathed in the Euphrates when dawns were young.
I built my hut near the Congo and it lulled me to sleep.
I looked upon the Nile and raised the pyramids above it.
I heard the singing of the Mississippi when Abe Lincoln went
   down to New Orleans, and I've seen its muddy bosom
   turn all golden in the sunset.

I've known rivers:
Ancient, dusky rivers.

My soul has grown deep like the rivers.[14]

footnotes

Roland Oliver and J. D. Fage, *A Short History of Africa*   **1**
(Baltimore, Penguin African Library, 1966), p. 14. Also,
Basil Davidson, *The Lost Cities of Africa* (Boston, Atlantic-Little, Brown and Co., 1959), pp. 4–6. Davidson,

Africa: History of A Continent (New York, Macmillan, 1966), pp. 13 ff.

John A. Williams, *Africa, Her History, Lands and People* **2** (New York, Cooper Square, 1962), pp. 7–8.

Davidson, *Africa,* pp. 128–141. **3**

Ibid., pp. 143–159. **4**

Oliver and Fage, *A Short History,* pp. 44–52 **5**

Davidson, *Lost Cities,* pp. 171–191. **6**

Africa Yesterday and Today, Clark D. Moore and Ann **7** Dunbar, eds. (New York, Bantam, 1968), pp. 121–126.

Davidson, *Africa,* pp. 83–94. (A map of principal trade **8** routes is on page 84).

Oliver and Fage, *A Short History,* pp. 112–134. **9**

Ibid., p. 126. **10**

Davidson, *Africa,* p. 177. **11**

Ibid., pp. 204–207. **12**

Davidson, *Lost Cities, pp.* 315–321. **13**

Hughes, *Selected Poems* (New York, Knopf, 1926). **14**

2

the negro: man with no past

So long,
So far away
Is Africa.
Not even memories alive
Save those that history books create . . .[1]

In his "Afro-American Fragment,"[2] the poet Langston Hughes celebrated Africa, but not the Africa of history books. We saw in the first chapter that much "history" about Africa is simply not true. And that brief sketch of African history is important for us in order to understand the rise of black consciousness in this country. Africa, and black consciousness relate directly to the problem of the Negro in America today: for the Negro is a man without a past, at least a past that he wants to admit to. We can investigate this problem by comparing the Negro with other nationalities.

All men want to be proud of their past. Italians point to the glory of Rome; Greeks praise Homer; the British speak of the Magna Carta and of Shakespeare, and so it is with every country. People desire and need this kind of pride. What about, however, the American Negro? What can he look back to? Only two things: Africa, and slavery.

Rejecting a Homeland

Up to very recent times, as the first chapter pointed out, Africa could hardly bring about a feeling of pride. This was surely not the fault of Africa, but rather a misreading of history. Westerners, judging the African culture in terms of their own, concluded that Africans were savages, inferior humans, children never grown up. Like the general public, African-Americans themselves believed this untruth, and subsequently separated themselves from all that was African. In doing so, they cut themselves off from a very precious heritage.

The second part of their history was one of slavery. These two words, Africans and slaves, contributed little towards establishing ethnic pride in origins. But, actually, they are a matter of great pride. We have seen, in chapter one, the falsity of regarding Africa as the "home of savages."[3] Later on, we will see how much there is of a proud tradition in the history of American black people even during their centuries of forced labor in this country.

First, let us look at the situation of the African-American who has cut himself off from his African background. "Surely," he or she unwittingly said to himself, "I don't want to be associated with one of those uncivilized African savages." So, the African-American sets out to identify himself with anything as long as it is non-African. He ends up imitating the white American, and thus becomes a "Negro."[4] And although it is common to see in our cities French berets, scotch plaid ties, Irish sweaters, Russian hats, and Indian saris, until very recently no one saw anything which hinted of Africa. Black Americans tried not to think that their ancestors came from the "dark continent."

This points to a loss of pride in one's origins, always an important factor in man's emotional life. Black Americans tried to act, speak, and even *look* like white

Americans. They tried to straighten their naturally kinky hair, lose their musical southern drawls, inhibit their sense of rhythm, and even lighten their skin!

History and a Homeland

All this is changing rapidly. Rather than be a matter of shame, African background is becoming a matter of pride. Rather than being played down, blackness is being emphasized. And a new sense of pride in origins runs through the younger generations of African-Americans. They are determined not to be "Negroes," but black men and black women. *Black is beautiful,* they say.

The second part of an African-American's heritage is slavery. In the past, this was thought of as something to be ashamed of. A new viewpoint comes to the forefront today, however, which would change this shame to pride. The cause for this change in attitude lies in the realization and admission, finally, that black labor played an invaluable role in building up the United States.

Although Europe began the market in African slaves, the American colonies made it a most successful business.[5] Populous Europe had little need for imported labor, but the sparsely settled colonies needed it desperately. Fields needed cultivation; who would cultivate them? And what about the mines, the railroad, construction—the countless tasks needed to make a wilderness into a new Europe? The chosen solution: get rid of the red man, and bring in the black man. Steal the red man's land and get the black man to cultivate it. These are harsh facts, but they are, sadly, true. For our purposes, however, they point out an important fact: the United States could never have grown strong without the muscles of Africans. The strength and size of this country owes unpaid debts to its black citizens. And although tributes have been given to the contributions of the Irish, the Poles, the Italians, and other nationalities, no tributes have been given to the Africans, whose forefathers were forced to work under subhuman conditions to build this nation up. The African-American of today sees the painful history of his ancestors: deportation from their homeland, slave ships where 15 percent died, breakdown in family ties, relegation to animal status, forced labor, the whole terror of slavery, and he says with great pride, "We must be a strong people to have survived."

These two together—national identity and history—spell the death toll of the American Negro, because the Negro is something invented by the white man.[6] The Negro remains in psychological slavery; that is, he still wants to imitate the white "masters" of society. A new voice cries out of the American melting pot, *we are black people, we are from Africa, and we are proud of it.*[7] The future goes in the direction of this voice; there is no turning back.

What will white America do without the Negro? White Americans will simply have to get used to black Americans, and allow them to be what they want to be. In the past, great social pressure weighed on black Americans to conform to the ideas of the whites. The conformists, those who try to please the whites, are called derogatively "white man's niggers," or "Uncle Toms."[8] The young-thinking black people today no longer want to be assimilated into American culture; rather, they want to become a part of it, with their own special identity and direction. They have given America much in the past, and they have received little thanks or recognition for it. They can give even more in the future; but it will be seen and recognized. The Negro is dead. Long live the black man.

The Imagined Negro

If you repeat a lie often enough, people will begin to believe you. The imagination of people in this country has been fed mountains of lies about African-Ameri-

cans. They have eaten, digested, and made these lies part of themselves and their outlook. Who fed them these lies? Those who shape imaginations through novels, poetry, films, radio, and television. Since they believed what they were told to believe, the imaginations of white America grew on caricatures, and not on authentic pictures. We can think of one example already—the savage in the jungle. All of us remember films or have read books about these half-animals in the forests who throw a barbaric banquet for the "great white hunter"; or who, perhaps, eat the hunter at the banquet. We have experienced the adventures of Tarzan, even the Lord of the Jungles had to be white. Songs speak of "the darkies"—happy, simpleminded folk so contented with their life on the plantation. *Amos and Andy,* a popular radio program, portrayed "typical Negroes" as lovable, friendly, cheerful, and quite dull-witted. Until recent years movies portrayed Negroes as house servants with big eyes, or shoeshine boys. Always, of course, "boy." Why not a heroic man, or a beautiful woman? The essential point is that the imaginations of Americans have been programmed to think of black people as inherently inferior. And Americans believed the lie; it was repeated to them often enough.

Even more tragic than this, however, is that many black people themselves have believed this lie! A black child in America is almost doomed to grow up with an inferiority complex *because he is black!* This is slavery of a psychological nature, a torturous kind of colonialism. A man becomes what he thinks of himself. Mass media in the past convinced many black Americans that they were inferior. Black spokesmen for today are rejecting that emphatically: "we shall view ourselves as African-Americans, determined, intelligent, beautiful, and peace-loving." This is the "new look" that black Americans are insisting for themselves. White America, listen!

"Outcast"

—Claude McKay

For the dim regions whence my fathers came
My spirit, bondaged by the body, longs.
Words felt, but never heard, my lips would frame;
My soul would sing forgotten jungle songs.
I would go back to darkness and to peace,
But the great western world holds me in fee,
And I may never hope for full release
While to its alien gods I bend my knee.
Something in me is lost, forever lost,
Some vital thing has gone out of my heart,
And I must walk the way of life a ghost
Among the sons of earth, a thing apart.

For I was born, far from my native clime,
Under the white man's menace, out of time.[9]

footnotes

Hughes, *Selected Poems.* **1**
Ibid. **2**
Davidson, *Lost Cities,* pp. 318–319; Richard Wright, **3**
White Man, Listen! (New York, Anchor, 1964), pp. 10–11;
Charles E. Silberman, *Crisis in Black and White* (New
York, Vintage, 1964), pp. 167–188.
Alvin F. Poussaint, "The Negro American: His Self-Image **4**
and Integration" in *The Black Power Revolt,* Floyd B.
Barbour, ed. (Boston, Extending Horizons Books, 1968),
pp. 94–103; William H. Grier and Price M. Cobbs, *Black
Rage* (New York, Basic Books, 1968), pp. 18–31; C. Eric
Lincoln, *Sounds of the Struggle* (New York, William
Morrow, 1968), p. 53.
Daniel P. Mannix, *Black Cargoes* (New York, Viking, **5**

1965), pp. 67–68; John Hope Franklin, *From Slavery to Freedom* (New York, Knopf, 1956), p. 45.

Lincoln, *Sounds,* p. 134. **6**

Adelaide Cromwell Hill, "What is Africa to Us?" in *Black* **7** *Power Revolt,* Barbour, ed., pp. 127–135; Silberman, *Crisis,* pp. 162–188.

Sterling Brown, "A Century of Negro Portraiture in Amer- **8** ican Literature," in *Black Voices,* Abraham Chapman, ed., pp. 564–567. Malcolm X speaks of the contemporary "Uncle Tom" in *The Autobiography of Malcolm X* (as told to Alex Haley) (New York, Grove Press, 1965), p. 243.

Selected Poems of Claude McKay (New York: Bookman **9** Associates, 1953. Used by permission of Twayne Publishers.)

3
three-fifths
of a man

The American dream has been painted with various shades of white. More color is needed. The American colonies, which promised refuge and freedom for the persecuted religious sects of England, held out neither to the imported labor from Africa. The same colonies which offered freedom from tyranny and oppression, in turn wrote one of the most tragic chapters in the world's history of tyranny and oppression. The great American dream is balanced by the great American puzzle: how political and religious refugees could fight and die for their own freedom, and yet be willing to deny that same freedom to another man. We shall have to investigate the causes which prompted men, and convinced them, that they should act in such a contradictory manner.

Africans were forcibly deported from their native land to work in the "new world," from as early as 1518.¹ The first sale of Africans in the English colonies took place at Jamestown in 1619 or 1620. American democracy grew up hand in hand with American slavery. A great nation was in the making, provided the red men moved out and the black men moved in. So often in this American epic the early years of colonization are portrayed as the sole accomplishment of white men—

those explorers, early settlers, pioneers, and statesmen whose names are so familiar to us. But it was not the accomplishment of white men alone; true, they received the most attention. But while they were in the limelight of history, the blacks were in the fields, showing a land how to grow crops; and the red men were in the forests, moving farther and farther away from the land they had always considered theirs. The job of laying the foundations for the future of the United States was a technicolor job and all the actors were necessary. We must make the "American dream" fit the multi-colored facts of history.

How did early Americans convince themselves to do such "split thinking," to free themselves and to enslave others? They were able to do this kind of thinking only by hiding the truth from themselves. The truth was that in this undeveloped land, before the coming of the machine, labor was desperately needed.[2] Even the steady flow of immigrants from England could not fill the ever increasing job openings. They turned to forced labor, which included blacks and whites,[3] as a convenient way out.

A bonded servant at that time agreed to work for a number of years in return for passage to the colonies and room and board. At the end of the contract, the bonded man or woman became free to build an independent life. At least in the beginning, this possibility of freedom seemed to have been extended to blacks. But by the 1660s, colonial laws arose extending African-Americans' term of bondage to their entire lives and to their children also. The blacks had no defense; their opinion was not asked. So, we see that one hundred years before the *Declaration of Independence* that same dream of independence was taken away from a large segment of the American population. Men and women fled Europe only to plant a few decades later even greater injustices in the new world. We can say that the very roots of American democracy were diseased.

Besides the desperate need for labor, another reason prompting colonists to do "split thinking" was that the blacks were, relatively speaking, defenseless people. This does not mean they were weak, or accepted the white man's yoke without a struggle; the history of their rebellions demonstrates this. But they were defenseless. They could appeal to no polls, or voting processes; public opinion in those days remained stable, uninfluenced by mass-media newspapers, television, radio, and films. The Africans, transplanted to a foreign land and language, deprived of national, tribal, and family ties, everything which gave them power over their environment, and even, finally, deprived of their manliness and womanliness, were indeed defenseless. They were on the lowest rung of the colonial "pecking order."

A need for labor, combined with the people who could not defend themselves, dulled the consciences of our American forefathers so that they not only came to accept the enforced slavery of other men, but tried to convince themselves that it was right and proper. One thinks here of the Nazi regime in Germany that slaughtered millions of Jews for reasons they thought right and proper. "Man's inhumanity to man" is so often accomplished by sincere people.

How did the early settlers of the colonies justify their "split thinking"—freedom for themselves, slavery for others? Basically they used three arguments. First of all, they said, the black man is inferior to the white man.[4] We can even say they had to think this way in order to justify, in their own minds, their conduct. Its objective truth is another matter, of course. Take a person from his familiar environment, place him in a foreign climate with a strange language and people; strip him of dignity, and then be convinced that he is "inferior" to yourself. We can trace such fuzzy reasoning to the false "superiority complex" Europeans have been suffering from. It is interesting to speculate what would be the case if the tables were turned, and a colonist were taken to Africa, placed in the midst of a strange environment, language, and people, and chained, whipped, and sold to the highest black bidder who had power of life and death over him.

There was nothing "inferior" about African-Americans, except the treatment they received by Europeans. We have seen how, collectively, the African people came to answer the challenges of their native land, and succeeded in building up peaceful, prosperous, and even enviable civilizations.

Another reason used to attempt to justify slavery was the belief that the Africans brought to this country were already slaves in their native land. This brings up the question of slavery as practiced in Africa.

There is some truth in saying that the original Africans sold to Europeans and, later, Americans were already slaves in Africa.[5] The institution as found in Africa differed greatly from its later development in the Americas. Bondage in Africa was on a limited scale, the result of tribal skirmishes, debt, or other social violations. Its pattern formed part of the social makeup and did not include the absolute loss of human dignity later found in the new world's brand of slavery. Even though the first Africans taken as slaves were already in bondage, this soon proved inadequate to fill the ever-increasing demand from the growing colonies. Soon, raids upon neighbors were made, with the help of European firearms, in order to supply the demanded human commodity. No, the colonists were wrong: Africans taken to this country were not slaves; they were free men and free women in their own land who found themselves one day, suddenly dispossessed of their homes, families, land, and even identities. Their future destiny: to live as slaves in the land of freedom.

This brings us to perhaps the most pernicious of

all reasons to justify slavery—religion. Throughout history it has been noted that men will use the most exalted reasons to justify their most base actions. American attitudes towards Africans fall into this classification. Scripture was quoted to cite examples of slavery in biblical times; the black man was said to be under the curse of Noah's son Ham;[6] and finally, that these Africans were actually being benefited by enjoying the opportunity of baptism and "civilization!"[7]

Today we can easily reject the reasons popular in colonial days to justify slavery—inferiority, or the advantages of baptism and a "civilized society." Our simple rejection of this kind of thinking, however, does not erase the brutal facts that perhaps millions of Africans died in slave ships coming to this country.[8] As Robert Hayden, a black poet, expressed it:

from "Middle Passage"

> voyage through death
> > to life upon these shores
>
> "10 April 1800—
> Blacks rebellious. Crew uneasy. Our linguist says their moaning is a cry for death, ours and their own. Some try to starve themselves. Lost three this morning leaped with crazy laughter to the waiting sharks, sang as they went under."[9]

As for the millions who reached this country, little of the "American dream" greeted them, except the doubtful privilege of building up a white man's country. In the Constitution of the United States (Article 1, Section 2, clause 3) they were classified as "three-fifths of a man."[10]

Representatives and direct Taxes shall be apportioned among the several States which may be included within this Union, according to their respective Numbers, which shall be determined by adding to the whole Number of free Persons, including those bound to Service for a Term of Years, and excluding Indians not taxed, three fifths of all other Persons . . .

How can we wonder today that the African-Americans of this land feel themselves without meaningful roots? The popular American epic of history books, of the movies, and of television programs doesn't include Africans who were only counted as three-fifths of a person at the time. Can a black teenager today feel any kind of patriotism when he reads of the exploits of Daniel Boone, or learns the terms of the Louisiana Purchase? Or even when he studies that Constitution which formed the basis for this nation, and the Bill of Rights which gave no rights to his ancestors?

The history of colonial slavery is not a disgrace for the black man; it is a disgrace for the white man. Despite our regard and respect for the pioneers who built this country, we must not overlook the fact that they compromised their own principles of freedom and liberty. Their "split-thinking" was not entirely honest.

The dream they had for this country was of one color only. Today it is the job of young-thinking America to change this thinking and this dream. Americans must dream in technicolor—white, yellow, black, brown, and red. Variety is the spice of life, and it is the life of America.

"I Dream a World"

—Langston Hughes

I dream a world where man
No other will scorn,
Where love will bless the earth
And peace its paths adorn.
I dream a world where all
Will know sweet freedom's way,
Where greed no longer saps the soul
Nor avarice blights our day.
A world I dream where black or white,
Whatever race you be,
Will share the bounties of the earth
And every man is free,
Where wretchedness will hang its head,
And joy, like a pearl,
Attend the needs of all mankind.
Of such I dream—
Our world![11]

footnotes

1   Mannix, *Black Cargoes,* p. 3; John Hope Franklin, *From Slavery to Freedom,* pp. 49 ff.

2   Mannix, *Black Cargoes,* pp. xii–xiii; Franklin, *Slavery to Freedom,* pp. 47–49.

3   *Ibid.,* p. 70.

4   For Thomas Jefferson's views on "black inferiority" see Matthew T. Mellon, *Early American Views on Negro Slavery* (New York, Mentor, 1969), pp. 104–108.

5   Franklin, *Slavery,* p. 30.

6   *Chronicles of Negro Protest,* Bradford Chambers, ed. (New York, Parents' Magazine Press, 1968), pp. 17–20;

see also "David Walker's Appeal" in *Black Protest,*
Joanne Grant, ed. (New York, Fawcett, 1968), p. 85.

Chronicles, Chambers, ed., p. 33.   7

Mannix, *Black Cargoes,* pp. 104 ff.   8

Hayden, *Selected Poems* (New York, October House,   9
1966).

Civil Rights and the American Negro, Albert P. Blau-   10
stein and Robert L. Zangrando, eds. (New York, Washington Square, 1968), p. 49.

American Negro Poetry, Arna Bontemps, ed. (New York,   11
Hill and Wang, 1964), pp. 71–72.

4
the slave who fought back

Frederick Douglass, born a slave in 1817, learned there are two paths to freedom. First, find out what freedom is through education. The second path is to fight for it, and to use violence if necessary. His own life, especially his conduct throughout the Civil War, shows these beliefs.[1]

First of all, education. In Baltimore, when Frederick was about eight-years-old, Mrs. Auld, the wife of his "master," taught the young slave the letters of the alphabet. When her husband found out what she was doing, he became extremely angry, and ordered her not to continue. Besides being against the law, Auld said, it was even bad for the slave himself:

> A nigger should know nothing but to obey his master—to do what he is told. Learning would *spoil* the best nigger in the world. Now, if you teach that nigger how to read, there would be no keeping him. It would forever unfit him to be a slave. He would at once become unmanageable, and of no value to his master. As to himself, it could do him no good, but a great deal of harm. It would make him discontented and unhappy.[2]

From that moment, Frederick Douglass understood one path to freedom, and he took steps along this road. He understood that education and slavery were incompatible, and he made certain that he would be educated. He made friends with the white children in the neighborhood, and persuaded them to help him learn. Sometimes he would even bribe poor white children by giving them bread and food from the kitchen, to which he had easy access. He kept books secretly, and stole time from his errands in order to read them. Writing was a more difficult art to acquire, but the young slave even succeeded in doing this. His first lessons came from copying abbreviations for "starboard," "larboard," "aft," and "forward" from the crates in the shipyard. Thus he learned the letters "s," "l," "a," and "f" first; using these as a basis, he gradually learned how to write. And, as Mr. Auld predicted, the more Frederick learned, the more dissatisfied he became.

> The more I read, the more I was led to abhor and detest my enslavers. I could regard them in no other light than a band of successful robbers, who had left their homes, and gone to Africa, and stolen us from our homes, and in a strange land reduced us to slavery. I loathed them as being the meanest as well as the most wicked of men.[3]

Douglass' second road towards freedom came about through violent self-defense. In his sixteenth year his "owners" hired him out to a Mr. Covey. This man enjoyed a great reputation for "breaking slaves." He set out to break the spirit of Frederick, and almost succeeded. For the first six months, Covey whipped Douglass almost every week. His brutality knew no limits. One day Frederick collapsed at work. Covey came and asked what was the matter. Douglass relates this incident.

I told him as well as I could, for I scarce had strength to speak. He then gave me a savage kick in the side, and told me to get up. I tried to do so, but fell back in the attempt. He gave me another kick, and again told me to rise. I again tried, and succeeded in gaining my feet; but stooping to get the tub with which I was feeding the fan, I again staggered and fell. While down in this situation, Mr. Covey took up the hickory slat with which Hughes had been striking off the half-bushel measure, and with it gave me a heavy blow upon the head, making a large wound, and the blood ran freely; and with this again told me to get up.[4]

After this incident, Douglass left the Covey farm for a day and a night. When he returned, Covey again attacked him with violence. Then something happened inside the teen-ager; perhaps he realized his life depended on it or perhaps the education he had given himself returned strength into his almost-broken spirit. At any rate, he did not respond non-violently to Covey's attack. Douglass defended himself, and met force with force:

but at this moment—from whence came the spirit I don't know—I resolved to fight; . . . . I seized Covey hard by the throat; and as I did so, I rose. He held on to me, and I to him. My resistance was so entirely unexpected, that Covey seemed taken all aback. He trembled like a leaf. This gave me assurance, and I held him uneasy, causing the blood to run where I touched him with the ends of my fingers.[5]

This dramatic fight lasted for two hours. Douglass won and the slavemaster Covey lost. Douglass calls it the "turning point" in his "career" as a slave. This battle, he says, transformed him from a slave into a man. "It was a glorious resurrection, from the tomb of slavery, to the heaven of freedom. My long-crushed spirit rose, cowardice departed, bold defiance took its place."[6] From this time forward, Douglass never allowed himself to be whipped. Four years later he escaped and went to New York.

The Fight Continued

Douglass' battle did not end with Covey, or with his escape to freedom. He continued fighting for his cause from the lecture platform. In those days before radio, television, and movies, a powerful public speaker had great influence and Douglass was precisely this. He was a large, handsome man with an imposing voice. Moreover, he spoke from personal experience and intense conviction. In 1841, when he was twenty-four, the Massachusetts Anti-Slavery Society sponsored him as a speaker. His public career began, and Douglass, the former slave, became in time one of the most important men of the nineteenth century.

In just four years of lecturing, it was no longer safe for Douglass to stay in this country. He had built up a reputation as a speaker and writer. This latter distinction came about in 1845, when he published his *Narrative*,[7] telling his experiences as a slave. His identity then became known and since he was still a "fugitive slave," professional slave-catchers could have kidnapped him, and collected a reward for returning him to slavery. Douglass decided to leave the country. So, in 1845, he left on a speaking tour of Ireland and England. There, audiences continued to receive him with welcome. They responded to his appeals warmly. In fact, British friends raised enough money for him that he was able to "buy" his freedom legally, and eventually return in safety to the United States.

The North Star

"Agitate, agitate, agitate,"[8] Douglass once said to a young man who asked him for advice. These words guided the ex-slave throughout his own career. He returned from overseas not only with his legal freedom, purchased by English friends, but also with enough funds to start an anti-slavery newspaper. The platform of the paper was to be "a terror to evil doers." The first issue of the *North Star,* later changed to *Frederick Douglass' Paper,* appeared in 1847. It continued for the next sixteen years, published from Rochester, Douglass' headquarters.

In just a single decade, Douglass had risen from slave status to lecturer, writer, and publisher. His name was known on both sides of the Atlantic as a leader of reform. These were amazing accomplishments for a man who had once been whipped weekly as a "nigger" who "should know nothing but to obey his master." A sad realization stems from Douglass' rise and achievements. How many similar men of talent never reached freedom as he did, but instead lived their entire lives working as slaves? How much richer this country might be today if men of genius, like Douglass, had been given sufficient opportunity. Douglass himself, however, had been given little; he had to take education and freedom for himself. He said once that he was whipped oftenest who was whipped easiest."[9] Douglass simply did not allow himself to be whipped.

Political Background

The first political opponent Douglass met was his friend and first sponsor, William Lloyd Garrison. This famous abolitionist—calling for an immediate end to slavery—held that the Constitution itself promoted slavery, and therefore, all political activity was of no use. Douglass agreed with Garrison's anti-slavery campaign, but felt that involvement in politics, especially voting, was of prime importance. A split with Garrison developed, which was complete by 1851. Douglass wanted to be no man's disciple.

During these years, the Liberty Party rose in America. Organized in the early 1840s to oppose slavery, it naturally attracted Douglass to its ranks. But, like other small parties, it functioned to influence larger parties rather than to win elections. By 1860, it—and other small parties—had done considerable work. The country reached a climax of tension the year before by the execution of John Brown. This man had attempted to lead slaves in a revolt against the South. He roused much anti-slavery feeling by words like these:

> You may dispose of me easily, but this question is still to be settled—the Negro question—the end of that is not yet. Now if it is deemed necessary that I should forfeit my life for the furtherance of the ends of justice, and mingle my blood with the blood of my children and with the blood of millions in this slave country whose rights are disregarded by wicked, cruel, and unjust enactments, I say, let it be done.[10]

It was done; Brown was executed, and he became a martyr to the cause of abolition. Douglass said of John Brown that he "began the war that ended slavery and made this a free republic."[11] The following year, Abraham Lincoln came to the Presidency on the Republican ticket.

Douglass and the War

The Civil War did not begin as a war against slavery; it began as a war against secession from the Union.[12] Douglass and other abolitionists wanted to turn it into a crusade against the institution of slavery. In this effort, they were frustrated for years, even by the "Great Emancipator" himself, Abraham Lincoln.

Although he ran on the Republican ticket, opposing the extension of slavery to the West, Lincoln was by no means an abolitionist. At most he favored gradual emancipation and the colonization of black Americans outside the borders of this country.[13] Besides this, he was anxious not to offend the "border states" by taking a strong anti-slavery stand. Douglass repeatedly criticized these policies of Lincoln, admitting that he was "bewildered by the spectacle of moral blindness, infatuation, and helpless imbecility which the government of Lincoln presents."[14] The President, for example, in the beginning of the war ordered that slaves who fled to Union armies should be returned to their owners; he overruled General Fremont's declaration of emancipation in Missouri;[15] he refused to allow black soldiers in the Union army.[16]

This latter point seemed essential to Douglass. Perhaps he remembered his own struggle against the slave-breaker Covey. At any rate, he believed that membership in the army was important for the future of the black man in America:

> Once let the black man get upon his person the brass letters, U.S.; let him get an eagle on his button and a musket on his shoulder and bullets in his pocket, and there is no power on the earth . . . which can deny that he has earned the right to citizenship in the United States.[17]

Finally, on January 20, 1863, Secretary of War Stanton authorized the governor of Massachusetts to raise two segregated regiments. His motives were not idealistic; rather, they were prompted by mounting losses, decline in white enlistments, and great opposition to the newly instituted draft. Popular opinion also changed. seeing that every black soldier enabled a white man to stay home. A jingle of the times expressed this idea:

> In battle's wild commotion
> I shouldn't at all object
> If Sambo's body should stop a ball
> That was coming for me direct.[18]

Nevertheless, Douglass saw the army as a "golden opportunity" for black men. In his famous editorial "Men of Color, To Arms," he wrote rousing words: "I urge you to fly to arms, and smite with death the power that would bury the government and your liberty in the same hopeless grave . . . ." Black Americans responded to this call, and paid dearly for "the right to citizenship in the United States."[19]

Almost 200,000 served in the Union forces; 18 percent of the North's freedmen enlisted, while only 7 percent of the whites did. Blacks took greater risks in fighting, because southern policy at first treated them as rebellious slaves, rather than as prisoners of war. Even the Union, in the beginning, only gave black soldiers half the pay of white soldiers. Thirty-eight thousand gave their lives for the Union cause. Douglass, working to enlist soldiers, objected to such inequality in pay and in treatment. He sought an audience with the President in July, 1863, and put forth his complaints. He went away from the interview convinced that Lincoln was "an honest man." By the end of the war, black soldiers received equal pay, and the North demanded they be treated as soldiers, and not as runaway slaves. Douglass' ideas prevailed. He believed in fighting hard for what he thought was right and just.

The Emancipation Proclamation

In effect, the "Emancipation Proclamation" did not free anyone. Lincoln likewise did not issue it out of hatred for slavery, but primarily as a war measure. In the document itself he called it "a fit and necessary war measure for suppressing said rebellion," and he justified his action by "military necessity." He issued it only eighteen months after the war began, because as he stated: "Things have gone from bad to worse, until I felt we had reached the end of our rope . . . ." He regarded the proclamation as a "last card"[20] in the war effort. By it he meant to threaten the South: if they did not stop fighting within one hundred days, he declared their slaves "are and henceforward shall be free."[21] By this threat of a rebellious black population within enemy lines, the President hoped peace would come about. Significantly, the proclamation applied to slaves only within enemy territory; it did not apply to slaves within states faithful to the Union, nor even in Southern states occupied by Union armies.

The President issued the proclamation on September 22, 1862; the next one hundred days expired and the Confederacy did not stop the war. So, the proclamation became effective on the first day of the new year. Although Douglass recognized the weaknesses in the document, he called it the "deathblow" to the "slave holding rebellion." It was surely a moment of triumph in Douglass' life, one which he had worked towards ever since he learned the alphabet and defended himself against the "slave-breaker" Auld.

In the decades to come, Douglass would have many other battles on his hands, which he would not avoid. Unfortunately at his death in 1895, he realized that his dreams had not been accomplished. Instead of a harmonious nation working for justice and equality, he saw his own people "torn from their little cabins, snatched from jails by furious mobs with no chance to prove their innocence of the crime imputed to them, shot down, hanged and burned to death."[22] At the time of his death, numerous states were moving to deprive black citizens of the vote. Riots, lynchings, and race hatred were ordinary news for Americans. Yet, as early as 1866, Douglass warned that the Civil War might become "a miserable failure, barren of permanent results, —a scandalous and shocking waste of blood and treasure . . . of no value to liberty or civilization." In many ways his prophecy came true. His vision, however, remains, perhaps for a new generation of Americans to accomplish.

"Frederick Douglass"

—Robert Hayden

When it is finally ours, this freedom, this liberty, this beautiful
and terrible thing, needful to man as air,
usable as earth; when it belongs at last to our children,
when it is truly instinct, brain matter, diastole, systole,
reflex action; when it is finally won; when it is more
than the gaudy mumbo jumbo of politicians:
this man, this Douglass, this former slave, this Negro
beaten to his knees, exiled, visioning a world
where none is lonely, none hunted, alien,
this man, superb in love and logic, this man
shall be remembered. Oh, not with statues' rhetoric,
not with legends and poems and wreaths of bronze alone,
but with the lives grown out of his life, the lives
fleshing his dream of the beautiful, needful thing.[23]

footnotes

Benjamin Quarles, *Frederick Douglass* (New York, 1
Atheneum, 1968); Langston Hughes and Milton Meltzer,
A Pictorial History of the Negro in America (New York,

Crown Publishers, rev. ed., 1963), pp. 114 ff.

Frederick Douglass, *Narrative* (New York, Signet, 1968), p. 49.   2

Ibid., p. 55.   3

Ibid., p. 78.   4

Ibid., p. 83.   5

Quarles, *Douglass,* pp. 34–37, p. 337. This *Narrative*   6
was later enlarged by Douglass, and published in 1892, shortly before his death. See *Life and Times of Frederick Douglass, The Complete Autobiography* (New York, Collier, 1962).

Frederick Douglass, *Narrative* (New York: Signet, 1968).   7

Quarles, *Douglass,* p. x.   8

Written in an open letter addressed to President   9
Andrew Johnson. *Chronicles,* Chambers, ed., p. 150.

Civil Rights and the American Negro, Albert P. Blau-   10
stein and Robert L. Zangrando, eds. (New York, Washington Square, 1968), p. 175.

Quarles, *Douglass,* p. 185.   11

Franklin, *Slavery to Freedom,* pp. 267–268.   12

Ibid., p. 277.   13

Quarles, *Douglass,* p. 192.   14

Ibid., p. 191.   15

Franklin, *Slavery to Freedom,* p. 273.   16

Quarles, *Douglass,* p. 209.   17

Ibid., p. 203.   18

Chronicles, Chambers, ed., p. 138.   19

Franklin, *Slavery to Freedom,* p. 297.   20

Civil Rights, Blaustein and Zangrando, ed., p. 201.   21

Quarles, *Douglass,* p. 318.   22

Hayden, *Selected Poems.*   23

5
death of the fourteenth and fifteenth amendments

"We have a future; everything is possible to us,"[1] Frederick Douglass proclaimed when the Fifteenth Amendment passed. Finally, the black man in America had the undeniable right to vote. But by the end of his long and distinguished career, Douglass learned that he spoke such words with false hope. Despite the guarantees of these amendments, many black men in the country had their vote taken away from them.

It was not the first time it happened in the country. Once before in history, black men had the right to vote, given them by constitutions written during the Revolutionary Period. Thus, free black citizens could vote in the states of Maryland, North Carolina, New York, and Pennsylvania. However, in time, these states took the right to vote away from blacks; after 1830, few free black men voted in the country.

Fighting for the Vote

Immediately after the Civil War, however, two forces began working towards giving the former slaves the vote: Frederick Douglass; and the Radical Republicans.

We can easily see why Douglass wanted the franchise given to black citizens; he always worked for equal civil rights. And he considered the vote so important that he said in 1865 that he saw "little advantage in emancipation without this [the vote]."[2] He traveled throughout the Union States, speaking in favor of giving the vote to black men. "Slavery is not abolished," he said, "until the black man has the ballott."[3]

The Radical Republicans wanted this also, but for political reasons. If the freed blacks had the vote, this would help to keep the Democrats out of power. The Radical Republicans were certainly interested in doing this.

Black voting power was not easy to achieve. President Andrew Johnson, like Lincoln before him, opposed it. Johnson— "no friend of our race,"[4] said Douglass—claimed that giving the vote to freed slaves would only increase racial hatred in the South. His opponents maintained that only the vote would help make peace, by giving equal civil rights.

Northern feeling and Congress itself turned against the policies of Johnson. The "Black Codes" of the South (1865–66)[5] and new outbreaks of violence made the North determined to push through reforms whether the South liked them or not.

The "Black Codes," although raising blacks above slave status, did not make them free. In Louisiana, for example, a black worker could be fined one dollar—a large amount at the time—for "disobedience." This included many items, even leaving home without permission. Because of these codes, the anti-black violence, and Johnson's growing unpopularity, the elections of 1866 gave the Radical Republicans more than a two-thirds majority. They could, if they wished, even block a Presidential veto. They did this many times.

Andrew Johnson vetoed a bill in 1866 which gave the vote to black men in Washington, D.C.[6] Congress overrode his veto in three days.[7] Johnson vetoed the Reconstruction Act in 1867;[8] Congress again defeated his veto.[9] The Fourteenth Amendment passed in July, 1868. That year, thousands of blacks voted because of this amendment, and helped to make Grant, a Republican, the new President.

Supporters of black suffrage, however, still felt that the law was not clear enough. So, they wrote the Fifteenth Amendment, which explicitly gave the vote to all citizens. The states ratified this by 1870. This is when Douglass said, "Everything is possible to us!"[10]

Unequal Possibilities

Despite this, neither the North nor the South ever accepted the black citizen as first-class. They differed in methods: the North became more subtle than the South. Both, however, limited black citizens. And in the end, the North abandoned the cause of equality.

During Radical Reconstruction, however, a fight was waged to bring equality to the former slaves. Republicans divided the South into five military districts. These districts were ruled by the army until new constitutions were written, giving rights to blacks, and until the state ratified the Fourteenth Amendment. The states of the former Confederacy elected constitutional conventions, made up of both black and white representatives. The job of these conventions was to write new constitutions, and ratify the Fourteenth Amendment. Such terms of peace were difficult for white Southerners to accept, especially since Northern Radical Republicans demanded them.

Results, however, proved remarkable for the times. White men and black men composed new constitutions which for the first time in the South provided for public schools, hospitals, and homes for the physically handicapped. The conventions began repairing the destruction caused by the war.

Even during this reconstruction era, however, violence still prevailed in many areas. In 1871, for example, black citizens of Frankfort, Kentucky, sent a petition to Congress in which they wrote:

> We would respectfully state that life, liberty, and property are unprotected among the colored race of this state. Organized bands of desperate and lawless men mainly composed of soldiers of the late Rebel armies . . . have by force terror and violence subverted all civil society among colored people. . . . We believe you are not familiar with the description of the Klu Klux Klans riding nightly over the country going from county to county and in the county towns spreading terror wherever they go, by robbing, whipping, ravishing, and killing our people without provocation. . . .[11]

The petition listed sixty-four items, like "Silas Woodford age sixty badly beaten by disguised mob"; the list included forty-seven murders, twelve whippings, twelve beatings, and homes, a school, and a church destroyed. The citizens made an appeal to Congress "to enact some laws that will protect us."[12] Congress had tried to make such laws, but in the end the laws failed chiefly for three reasons: the North eventually lost interest in the cause; the South opposed the laws; the Supreme Court consistently voted against them.

The End of Reconstruction

Southern whites, having lost a war, certainly did not favor the terms of the Radical Reconstruction. They worked hard for the return of "home rule." The Democratic party of South Carolina, for example, said in 1876 that "every Democrat must feel honor-bound to control the vote of at least one Negro, by intimidation, purchase, keeping him away, or as each individual may determine, how he may best accomplish it."[13]

Later on, those same articles said, "A dead Radical is harmless."[14] The South worked hard to rid itself of the hated northern rule, both political and military. By 1876, Reconstruction had ended in every state except South Carolina, Louisiana, and Florida.

It was an important year—a Presidential election. The Democrat Tilden opposed Republican Hayes. The election was so close that it depended on the disputed returns of these three Southern states. A special committee was set up to decide the winner of the election. Rutherford B. Hayes, in private, assured southern leaders that if he were elected, he would withdraw all Federal troops from the South.[15] In 1877, Hayes was declared the winner, and in that same year he ordered the army out of the South.[16] Reconstruction, then, ended "with a deal." The North lost interest in the cause of the freed slaves. The Republican party decided it did not need their vote. And the South wanted to take care of its problems its own way.

Blind Justice

In our own times we see the Supreme Court taking up the defense of the Fourteenth and Fifteenth Amendments, demanding that they be observed. It was not so, however, in the time after the Civil War. The historian Rayford Logan makes this harsh judgment in his book *The Betrayal of the Negro:*

> Practically all the relevant decisions of the United States Supreme Court during Reconstruction and to the end of the century nullified or curtailed those rights of Negroes which the Reconstruction "Radicals" thought they had written into laws and into the Constitution.[17]

The Supreme Court, then, destroyed many rights which the black man had acquired, or thought he had acquired. The court consistently voted against the spirit of the amendments, and civil rights legislation.

One example happened in 1876. Black citizens held a meeting in Louisiana to discuss the coming state election. Whites broke up the meeting, and the Supreme Court said it was not a case it could handle, despite the Fourteenth Amendment![18] In its *United States* versus *Cruikshank* case, the court said it could punish offenders only if the election discussed had been a national one.[19] In such cases, the court decided that states should handle the case. The Supreme Court also gave statements which upheld segregation in interstate transportation. This led to the complete "Jim Crow" separation of the white and black races in the South. Such separation happened, supported by law, by the beginning of the 1900s. The Supreme Court, then, failed as a friend to the black man, when such friendship was crucial for his future in the United States.

Silencing the Black Vote

By the end of the last century, all necessary preparations to take the vote away from black citizens had been made: the federal government was persuaded to let the states "do things their own way";[20] the Supreme Court showed that it would not defend the black man; the Republican party decided it didn't need the black vote; and white-power violence was determined to eliminate any dissenting voices. At that time—the 1890s—the great majority of black Americans lived in southern states. The anti-black battle was waged there; later on, the campaign would switch to the North.

In about twenty years, the constitutions of southern states, drawn up in Reconstruction times, were changed, in order to deprive the black man of the vote. Various ways of doing this were used: poll taxes, "literacy" tests (administered by whites), primaries limited to white voters, anything to get by the Fourteenth and Fifteenth amendments. These changed constitutions were designed to take away the vote from as many blacks as possible, as Senator J. K. Vardman of Mississippi said:

> I am just as opposed to Booker Washington as a voter, with all his Anglo-Saxon re-enforcements, as I am to the coconut-headed, chocolate-colored, typical little coon, Andy Dotson, who blacks my shoes every morning. Neither is fit to perform the supreme function of citizenship.[21]

The program to disenfranchise blacks was most successful. In Louisiana, for example, in 1896 there were 130,344 registered black voters.[22] Four years later, after the constitutional amendments, the number was down to 5,320.[23] In Alabama only 3,000 registered voters remained out of 181,471.[24] In effect, blacks in these states lost all political power. They were now in political slavery, rather than plantation slavery. Civil War would be needed to free them again.

Quarles, *Frederick Douglass,* p. 251. **1**

Ibid., p. 224. **2**

Speech delivered before the 32nd Annual Convention **3**
of the Americvan Anti-Slavery Society. Chambers, ed.,
Chronicles, p. 144.

Ibid., p. 147. **4**

Black Protest, Grant, ed., pp. 148–154. Benjamin **5**
Quarles, *The Negro in the Making of America* (New
York, Collier, 1964), pp. 129–131. *Civil Rights,* Blaustein
and Zangrando, eds., pp. 217–225.

Quarles, *Frederick Douglass,* p. 235. **6**

Ibid., p. 235. **7**

Kenneth M. Stampp, *The Era of Reconstruction, 1865–* **8**
1877 (New York, Vintage, 1967), p. 144.

Ibid., p. 144. **9**

Quarles, *Frederick Douglass,* p. 251. **10**

Black Protest, Grant, ed., p. 155. **11**

Ibid., p. 155. **12**

Chronicles, Chambers, ed., p. 160. **13**

Ibid., p. 161. **14**

Rayford W. Logan, *The Betrayal of the Negro* (New **15**
York, Collier, Enlarged Edition, 1965), p. 26.

Ibid., p. 31. **16**

Ibid., p. 105. **17**

Civil Rights, Blaustein and Zangrando, eds., p. 255. **18**

Ibid., pp. 256–258. **19**

Stampp, *Era of Reconstruction,* pp. 210–211. **20**

Elliot M. Rudwick, *W. E. B. DuBois* (New York, Athe- **21**
neum, 1968), p. 181.

Franklin, *Slavery to Freedom,* p. 337. **22**

Ibid., p. 337. **23**

Ibid., p. 337. **24**

6
the negro
moses

As the twentieth century began, a new generation of black Americans had been born—ones who had never known slavery. Since childhood, they had heard they were free men. Perhaps their fathers fought in the Civil War to make freedom and a united country a reality. After the terrors of that war, some men began to dream of a country where all would be equal under the law. In 1870, when the states ratified the Fifteenth Amendment, 20,000 black citizens of Baltimore heard slave-born Frederick Douglass say to them with confidence: "We have a future; everything is possible to us."[1]

Unfortunately, as time passed, black citizens learned that everything was *not* possible to them. Although declared free men, this generation of black people saw their freedoms constantly narrowing. The historian Benjamin Quarles calls the time after 1870 the "Decades of Disappointment."[2]

The reasons for disappointment added up as the years went on. Black Americans came to the brutal realization that society seemed determined to keep them "in their place," that is, third-class citizens, behind even the most recently arrived (white) immigrant from Europe. Society made sure that everything would not be possible for blacks: segregated schools remained inferior; unions refused membership; "Jim Crow"³ laws separating the races deprived blacks from even the ordinary dignities accorded men; the courts constantly disappointed them; the North, once the champion of the slaves, now worshipped the dollar sign. By the beginning of this century, after the "Decades of Disappointment," the black American's situation had hardly improved in twenty-five years. In fact, it was getting worse: "Jim Crow" laws increased; lynchings became ordinary headlines, and the ruling white classes in the South systematically prevented black Americans from using the vote. The freedom so ardently dreamed of never came. Instead, slavery was exchanged for third-class citizenship. Leadership and new directions were needed desperately. Into this leadership vacuum came two men who competed with each other: Booker T. Washington and W.E.B. DuBois. Their battle with ideas and with leadership influences even the thinking of the present day.

Up from Slavery

The man eventually called the "Black Moses"⁴ was born the son of a slave woman and a white father. The Civil War ended when he was about nine years old. Overcoming tremendous odds, the sixteen-year-old Booker T. Washington· entered Hampton Normal and Agricultural Institute in Virginia. The training he received there determined many of his later ideas, which he gave in abundance to the white and black audiences who heard him. Washington's education at Hampton was more industrial than intellectual. Students learned vocational skills such as carpentry, plumbing, building, and cooking. Washington became an outstanding product of Hampton, and in 1881, the principal of the Institute recommended him to found a new school in Alabama, *Tuskegee,* later called the "capitol of Negro America."⁵

Forty students enrolled in the new school, which

held classes at first in a church. With poorly prepared students, with opposition from the white community, inadequate facilities, and lack of money, Washington's task was huge. He determined to put into practice what he had experienced at Hampton; soon his students were learning not only to read and write, but to farm, to build, and to take care of themselves as completely as possible. Washington's ideal was this "industrial education."[6] Later on, many critics would attack him for this; however, we can hardly doubt that a great need existed for this kind of practical learning. His work progressed as he learned to fill the needs of his students, and yet to avoid offending the white ruling class. At all costs, he wanted to placate the whites, ardently believing in this working arrangement:

> Any movement for the elevation of the
> Southern Negro in order to be successful,
> must have to a certain extent the coopera-
> tion of the Southern whites. They control
> government and own the property. . . .[7]

Just why did southern and northern whites support "industrial education" so ardently? Surely a need existed to train the masses of freed men in the arts of living and making a sound economy for themselves. If the country applauded Washington's efforts in this from unselfish motives, we might look back to this period with pride. Unfortunately, the motives hardly seem unselfish. We sense a feeling of relief among white supporters of Washington's "industrial education" that the black man was being taught to *labor* rather than to *think.* This country had always wanted the labor of black men's bodies, but not of their minds. After 1877, with increased violence and insistence, white racism seemed determined to "keep the nigger in his place."[8] Charles Silberman, author of *Crisis in Black and White,* comments on this, speaking of the South:

The one sure way for the Negro to lose favor—in rural areas, to place himself in jeopardy—was to show signs of ambition: that is, to seek to rise above his "place."
. . . so long as a Negro remembered his place and acted obsequiously enough, the white man was ready to excuse—indeed to expect—laziness, indolence, inefficiency, and a certain amount of petty thievery.[9]

Real intellectual education would have upset this caste system or pecking order. So we see many whites viewing with approval Washington's efforts at "industrial education." Through such a program, the black man would fit neatly into the white man's system.

The Atlanta Compromise

By 1895, Booker T. Washington had become so popular that an invitation came to him, asking him to address the Cotton States Exposition in Atlanta. Author Arna Bontemps wrote that "A Negro on the platform of this southern city for an occasion like this? The whole nation would have its eyes on Atlanta that day."[10] Washington knew his delicate situation and above all he did not wish to offend anyone. The resulting speech drew unbelievable praise, made national headlines, put Washington in the position of leadership, and made W.E.B. DuBois later accuse Washington of making the "Atlanta Compromise."[11]

Addressing his fellow black Americans, Washington told them that: "It is at the bottom of life we must begin, and not at the top." He praised industrial education: "we shall prosper as we learn to dignify and glorify common labor and put brains and skill into the common occupations of life." To his white hearers, he spoke for the Negro: "In our humble way," he said, "you can be sure in the future, as in the past, that you and your families will be surrounded by the most patient, faithful, law abiding, and unresentful people that the world has ever seen." Washington even seemed to justify segregation by saying: "In all things that are purely social we can be as separate as the fingers, yet one as the hand in all things essential to human progress."[12]

The speech brought thunderous applause from the audience and from the nation. Washington was called "a safe leader";[13] congratulations poured in, even from President Cleveland. Assurances of financial support came, with appeals to give more speeches. The white world immediately recognized Booker T. Washington as the spokesman for the Negro race. He said what the white world wanted to hear.

Mistaken Logic

History has not been kind to Booker T. Washington. His "humble way" of friendship simply did not work. Its failure lay in a false assumption: that the white classes were willing to give black Americans full equality, but only gradually. Such was not the case, gradually or otherwise, as history shows. Washington depended on good will; it did not exist. Even as he spoke about the "patient, sympathetic help of my race"[14] the South Carolina convention was in session to take the vote away from the "patient, sympathetic" black man. On the same day as his speech, the leading southern paper—*Picayune* of New Orleans—reported an "Unsuccessful Lynching Bee" in Memphis. Within five years, Louisiana was to take the vote away from the black citizen; and North Carolina, Virginia, and Alabama also made evident plans to disenfranchise him. Only one year later, the same year Washington received an honorary degree from Harvard, the Supreme Court ruled *in favor of segregation* in the case of *Plessy* versus *Ferguson*.[15] The

white world applauded Washington, while they thrust the black man into a more and more subordinate position in society.

Nevertheless, Washington's reputation and influence grew even in the Negro community. Because of the support he received from wealthy industrialists like Andrew Carnegie, he became the most powerful Negro in America. "All roads led to Booker T. Washington."[16] He was known to three Presidents—McKinley, Taft, and Roosevelt. For the Negro community, this was called the "Age of Booker T. Washington."[17] He was consulted on almost every Negro appointment in education or in government. A letter of recommendation from him was a key to success in the Negro world, and sometimes in the white world also. Almost every Negro newspaper gave him support and praise. In 1911, Kelly Miller, a Negro sociologist, wrote to him: "You have the attention of the white world; you hold the pass-key to the heart of the great white race."[18] This surely seemed true, but opposition to the ideas and the methods of Booker T. Washington had been growing in his own camp. Whatever his relationship to the white race, Washington did not have the key to the hearts of the great black race.

footnotes

Quarles, *The Negro in the Making of America,* p. 138. 1

Ibid., p. 126. 2

Civil Rights, Blaustein and Zangrando, eds., pp. 283–322. 3
Also C. Vann Woodward, *The Strange Career of Jim Crow* (New York, Galaxy, 1957). For the origin of the term "Jim Crow" see *Chronicles,* Chambers, ed., p. 195. Also Hughes and Meltzer, *Pictorial History,* pp. 38–39.

Later on, this same term would be used also for Marcus **4**
Mosiah Garvey. See Edmund D. Cronon, *Black Moses:
The Story of Marcus Garvey* (Madison, University of
Wisconsin Press, 1962). For the term applicable to
Booker T. Washington, see Arna Bontemps, *100 Years
of Negro Freedom* (New York, Dodd, Mead, 1961),
p. 213.

Rudwick, *W. E. B. DuBois,* p. 87. **5**

100 Years, Bontemps, ed., pp. 88–105 relate the founda- **6**
tion and the purpose of Tuskegee. Also, Rudwick,
W. E. B. DuBois, pp. 60–62.

Ibid., p. 101. **7**

Stampp, *Era of Reconstruction,* p. 211. **8**

Silberman, *Crisis,* p. 96. **9**

100 Years, Bontemps, ed., p. 169. **10**

See "Of Mr. Booker T. Washington and Others" in Du **11**
Bois' *The Souls of Black Folk* (New York, Fawcett,
1961), pp. 42–55.

Chronicles, Chambers, ed., pp. 186–190. **12**

100 Years, Bontemps, ed., p. 173. **13**

Chronicles, Chambers, ed., p. 189. **14**

Civil Rights, Blaustein and Zangrando, eds., pp. 294–311. **15**

Quarles, *The Negro in the Making of America,* p. 167. **16**

Franklin, *Slavery to Freedom,* p. 390. **17**

Quarles, *The Negro in the Making of America,* p. 168. **18**

7

the problem of the twentieth century

Mr. Washington represents in Negro thought the old attitude of adjustment and submission. . . . It has been claimed that the Negro can survive only through submission. . . . As a result of this . . . palm branch, what has been the return? In these years have occurred:
1. The disenfranchisement of the Negro.
2. The legal creation of a distinct status of civil inferiority for the Negro.
3. The steady withdrawal of aid from institutions for the higher training of the Negro.

These movements are not, to be sure, direct results of Mr. Washington's teachings; but his propaganda has, without a shadow of a doubt, helped their speedier accomplishment.[1]

The battle against the "submission" philosophy of Booker T. Washington made a deliberate advance in 1903. In that year, W.E.B. DuBois published his book *The Souls of Black Folk.* James Weldon Johnson, the poet, said this book had "a greater effect upon and within the Negro race in America than any other single book published in this country since *Uncle Tom's Cabin.*"[2]

One of the chief effects of the book lay in its open criticism of Booker T. Washington. The attack came from a man with a far different background than the founder of Tuskegee.

W.E.B. DuBois

Washington spent his entire life in the South. W.E.B. DuBois, however, came from Massachusetts. Washington was born a slave; DuBois' family had been free men for generations. The family was among the oldest residents of the Great Barrington area, where DuBois was born. The education of Booker T. Washington consisted of some years at Hamstad. DuBois, on the other hand, took a doctorate degree from Harvard, and also studied in Germany.

From even so brief a contrast between the two men, we can see how Washington and DuBois would differ. A southerner and former slave, whose only degrees were honorary, would be more anxious to please the whites than would an American aristocrat such as DuBois. This latter man had more background, education, and intelligence than 90 percent of the people in this country. Yet he saw those same people move political machines in order to disenfranchise men like himself, make them a subservient caste, and paint on a belittling "Jim Crow" sign. DuBois naturally found accommodation harder to accept than Washington did. He had little choice but to take up an opposing flag to the speaker of the "Atlanta Compromise." There were many who followed him, mostly among the black intellectuals of the country.

Rumblings against the Washington philosophy had been heard for some years. Already in 1898, Paul Lawrence Dunbar, a black poet and a friend of Washington, was forced to criticize Tuskegee's "industrial education."

> Anyone who has visited the school at Tuskegee, Alabama, and seen the efficiency of the work being done there, can have no further doubt of the ability and honesty of purpose of its founder and president. But I do fear that this earnest man is not doing either himself or his race full justice in his public utterances. He says we must have industrial training, and the world quotes him
>
> > as saying
> > we must have
> > nothing else.[3]

The loudest opponent of Washington's leadership was William Monroe Trotter, also a Harvard graduate. Trotter published the Boston *Guardian*, considered the newspaper which spoke for the radical voice. For years, Trotter opposed the rising influence of Booker T. Washington's policy of white appeasement. The *Guardian* attacked Booker T. Washington from its first issues: "This man (Washington), whatever good he may do, has injured and is injuring the race far more than he can aid it. . . ."[4]

Trotter looked for a black leader whose voice would oppose the message of Washington. He had known DuBois at Harvard. As he watched the rising reputation of DuBois in educational circles, and read *The Souls of Black Folk*,[5] he thought he had finally found the man needed to speak to black Americans. In time, an alliance between the two men came about. After trying unsuccessfully to talk with the Booker T.

Washington camp, they went ahead and formed their own organization.

The Niagra Conference

At this time DuBois believed in the "talented tenth,"[6] that is, those men who have the greatest abilities for intelligence and leadership. He felt these men determined the future. For this reason, he opposed Washington's industrial education, if it neglected the education of the mind. His hope for the future of his race lay in its most intelligent leaders. He did not consider Booker T. Washington one of these.

So, in 1905, he invited a small group of the "talented tenth" to Niagara to found an opposing organization. Ironically, because of racial discrimination, the group had to meet on the Canadian side of the Falls.[7] There, they laid the groundwork for a black voice much different than Booker T. Washington's. Included among the demands they made were an end to "Jim Crow" segregation customs and laws, the right to vote, the right to work within labor unions, and the academic education of the "talented tenth."[8]

This activist program directly opposed Washington's, which always advised patience and gradualism. Washington recognized this, and one writer says he "scrutinized the movement and plotted its destruction."[9]

Nevertheless, the voice of loud protest had been raised in the Niagara Conference and from this point onward it would never cease:

> We refuse to allow the impression to remain that the Negro American assents to inferiority, is submissive under oppression, and apologetic before insults. Through helplessness we may submit, but the voice of protest of ten million Americans must never cease to assail the ears

of their fellows, so long as America is un-
just.[10]

The Niagara movement never became a mass
organization. Reasons for this varied: Washington's opposition surely had much to do with limiting its growth;
the message of loud protest was new, even to black
Americans; its appeal was mainly to the intellectual;
and even personal difficulties among the leaders prevented its growth. However, in a way, it gave birth to
a newer organization. This one, the National Association for the Advancement of Colored People, became
much larger and more powerful than the earlier Niagara Movement. In the decades which followed, the
NAACP played an important role in the advancement
of black consciousness.

Birth of the NAACP

White power, not black, has been the dominating force
in this country, as the following incident shows. It happened just a year before the one hundredth anniversary of Lincoln's birth: it happened just a few miles
from his tomb.

> The town officials saw that the mob
> was becoming unruly and several unsuc-
> cessful efforts were made to disperse it.
> Finally the Governor called out the militia.
> The mob, oblivious to the appeals of high
> state officials to respect the law, raided
> second-hand stores, secured guns, axes,
> and other weapons, and began to destroy
> Negro businesses and to drive Negroes
> from their homes. They set fire to a build-
> ing in which a Negro owned a barber shop.
> The barber was lynched in the yard be-
> hind his shop, and the mob, after dragging
> his body through the streets, was prepar-

ing to burn it when the militia from Decatur dispersed the crowd by firing into it. On the following night an 84-year-old Negro, who had been married to a white woman for more than 30 years, was lynched within a block of the State House. Before order was restored more than 5,000 militia men were patrolling the streets. In the final count, 2 Negroes had been lynched, 4 white men had been killed, and more than 70 persons had been injured. More than 100 arrests were made and approximately 50 indictments were returned. The alleged leaders of the mob went unpunished.

The news of the riot was almost more than Negroes could bear. It seemed to them a perverse manner in which to celebrate the one hundredth anniversary of the birth of Lincoln. Negroes were actually lynched within half a mile of the only home Lincoln ever owned and within two miles of his final resting place. Their cup was filled, and they hardly had the voice to cry out against this most recent outrage. It was time for drastic action. Somehow, some solution must be found to the problem of color, which DuBois had already called the greatest problem of the twentieth century.[11]

Drastic action never came, but alarmed people searched for a solution. It came in the form of a new organization—the NAACP. The idea for this originated with white citizens concerned about the latest outburst of racism in the country. They chose the one hundredth anniversary of Lincoln's birth as the founding date for their group. Oswald Villard, grandson of the abolitionist William Lloyd Garrison, challenged the country with these words: "We call upon all believers in democracy to join in a national conference for the discussion of present evils, the voicing of protests, and the renewal of the struggle for civil and political liberty."[12]

Booker T. Washington did not take part in the movement. DuBois, however, joined its executive committee, and took charge of publicity and research. In November, 1910, he published the first issue of the organization's newspaper, *The Crisis.* Under his leadership, this paper achieved a major voice in the growth of black awareness, reaching a circulation of more than 100,000 in less than ten years.

The NAACP took over where the Niagara movement failed. The presence of DuBois, however, insured some continuity between the two organizations. The NAACP—bringing the power of influential whites into the black movement—surely brought needed strength. But in this very strength lay weakness, because a white-black coalition, no matter how sincere, can never speak from a purely black standpoint.

Today we view the NAACP as a "moderate" organization. But at the time of its founding, it was not looked at this way. Any group speaking a different line of thought than Washington's patience and gradualism was considered radical. The NAACP declared its aim was to "make 11,000,000 Americans physically free from peonage, mentally free from ignorance, politically free from disenfranchisement, and socially free from ignorance."[13] These were strong words in 1910, when over seventy persons were lynched that year.

But the call, at least, had been sounded. A group of men—black and white—stood up in the tradition of the pre-war abolitionists. Slavery had gone, but freedom had not come yet for America's black minority. The Niagara Movement and the NAACP took a different road from the one taken by Booker T. Washington. The black community in America has chosen this road —pointed out by DuBois—rather than the one which led to Tuskegee.

"Booker T. and W.E.B."

—Dudley Randall

"It seems to me," said Booker T.,
"It shows a mighty lot of cheek
To study chemistry and Greek
When Mister Charlie needs a hand
To hoe the cotton on his land,
And when Miss Ann looks for a cook,
Why stick your nose inside a book?"

"I don't agree," said W.E.B.,
"If I should have the drive to seek
Knowledge of chemistry or Greek,
I'll do it. Charles and Miss can look
Another place for hand or cook.
Some men rejoice in skill of hand,
And some in cultivating land,
But there are others who maintain
The right to cultivate the brain."

"It seems to me," said Booker T.,
"That all you folks have missed the boat
Who shout about the right to vote,
And spend vain days and sleepless nights
In uproar over civil rights.
Just keep your mouths shut, do not grouse,
But work, and save, and buy a house."

"I don't agree," said W.E.B.,
"For what can property avail
If dignity and justice fail?
Unless you help to make the laws,

They'll steal your house with trumped-up clause,
A rope's as tight, a fire as hot,
No matter how much cash you've got.
Speak soft, and try your little plan,
But as for me, I'll be a man."

"It seems to me," said Booker T.—

"I don't agree,"
Said W.E.B.[14]

footnotes

DuBois, *The Souls of Black Folk,* pp. 48–49.   1

Rudwick, *W.E.B. DuBois,* p. 68.   2

100 Years, Bontemps, ed., p. 183.   3

Ibid., p. 187.   4

Rudwick, *W.E.B. DuBois,* pp. 66–71.   5

DuBois, *The Souls of Black Folk,* p. 85.   6

Chronicles, Chambers, ed., p. 205.   7

Ibid., pp. 208–211.   8

Rudwick, *W.E.B. DuBois,* p. 98.   9

Black Protest, Grant, ed., p. 208.   10

Franklin, *Slavery to Freedom,* pp. 436–437.   11

Ibid., p. 438. Also, Bontemps, *100 Years,* p. 199.   12

Quarles, *The Negro in the Making of America,* p. 175.   13

Randall, *Booker T. and W.E.B.* (Detroit, Mich., Broad-   14
side Press, n.d.).

8
white power

The New York Times, in 1903, published this story, which took place in Belleville, Illinois:

> The mob hanged Wyatt to a telephone pole in the public square. Even while his body was jerking in the throes of death from the strangulation, members of the mob began building a fire at the bottom of the pole. The flames flared up and licked at the feet of the victim, but this did not satisfy the mob, and another and larger fire was started.

> When it had begun burning briskly, the Negro still half alive, was cut down, and after being covered with coal oil was cast into the fire. Moans of pain were heard from the half dead victim of the mob, and these served further to infuriate his torturers. They fell upon him with clubs and knives and cut and beat the burning body almost to pieces, and not until every sign of life had departed did they desist and permit the flames to devour the body.[1]

1619–1718   Millions of black men, women, and children

died in slave ships on the passage to America.[2]

1829   A three-day riot in Cincinnati forced one thousand blacks to leave the city.[3]

1830   A mob drove black citizens out of Portsmouth, Ohio.

1834   Mobs in Philadelphia wrecked the African Presbyterian Church, burned homes, and attacked blacks during a three-day riot.[4]

1839   An anti-black riot in Pittsburgh.[5]

1862   In New York, a group of black women and children who worked at a factory were attacked by white mobs.[6]

1863   In New York, during a four-day riot, the draft office was burned, and blacks were hanged from trees and lampposts.[7]

1866   In Memphis, during riots, 40 blacks were killed and 70 were wounded.[8]

1866   In New Orleans nearly 40 blacks were killed during riots.[9]

1876   White mobs attacked black militiamen in Hamburg, South Carolina, killing several trying to escape, and 5 more after capture.[10]

1892   Fifteen blacks were killed during election riots in Georgia. Riots also occurred in Virginia and North Carolina.[11]

1898   In Wilmington, North Carolina, 3 whites were wounded, 11 blacks were killed, and 25 blacks were wounded.[12]

1884–1900   There were 2500 lynchings.[13]

1900   Over 100 blacks were lynched.[14]

1900–1914   There were 1100 lynchings.[15]

1900–1931   There were 1886 lynchings.[16]

1904   Two blacks in Statesboro, Georgia, who were convicted of murder, were burned alive by mobs. Two black women were whipped for crowding white girls off the sidewalk. Another was whipped for riding a bicycle on the sidewalk, and a mother of a three-day-old infant was beaten, and her husband, killed.[17]

1904   In a Springfield, Ohio, riot there was a lynching and eight buildings were burned.[18]

1906   In Atlanta, Georgia, there were four days of rioting.

1908   Over 5,000 militiamen had to restore order in Springfield, Illinois, after disturbances in which two blacks were lynched, four whites were killed, and seventy persons were injured.[19]

1917   Thirty-eight blacks were lynched.[20] In East St. Louis, Illinois, 40 black citizens were killed in a riot.[21]

1918   Fifty-eight blacks were lynched. In Tennessee more than 3,000 persons answered a newspaper advertisement to come and see the burning of a "live Negro."[22]

1919   Over 70 blacks lynched in this year, among them ten soldiers still in uniform. Eleven black citizens were publicly burned alive.[23]

1919   During the summer, 25 race riots occurred in the country. The Chicago one lasted 17 days, leaving 15 whites and 23 blacks dead, 178 whites and 342 blacks injured, and more than 1,000 families left homeless due to burning and destruction. The riot began by the stoning and sub-sequent drowning of a young boy who acci-dently drifted, on his homemade raft, into a "white" section of the beach.[24]

1921　In Tulsa, Oklahoma, 9 whites and 21 blacks were killed.[25]

1943　In thirty hours of rioting, Detroit required 6,000 militia to restore order. Twenty-five blacks and nine whites were killed during the disorder.[26]

1957　Federal troops came to Little Rock to stop mob violence because nine black students had been admitted to a local high school.[27]

1962　Army troops were sent to Oxford, Mississippi, when James Meredith arrived to enroll at the University of Mississippi.[28]

This chronology of incidents hardly begins to document the violence done to the black minority of this country.[29] But it serves, at least, to demonstrate that the dominant philosophy of the United States has been white power. The rise of the black power concept in recent years comes perhaps in response to a real need.

"If We Must Die"

—Claude McKay

If we must die—let it not be like hogs
Hunted and penned in an inglorious spot,
While round us bark the mad and hungry dogs,
Making their mock at our accursed lot.
If we must die—oh, let us nobly die,
So that our precious blood may not be shed
In vain; then even the monsters we defy
Shall be constrained to honor us though dead!

Oh, Kinsmen! We must meet the common foe;
Though far outnumbered, let us show us brave,
And for their thousand blows deal one deathblow!
What though before us lies the open grave?
Like men we'll face the murderous, cowardly pack,
Pressed to the wall, dying, but fighting back![30]

footnotes

Rayford W. Logan, *The Betrayal of the Negro* (Collier Books), pp. 391–392. [1]

Franklin, *Slavery to Freedom,* pp. 56–58. [2]

Ibid., p. 232. [3]

Ibid., p. 232. [4]

Ibid., p. 232. [5]

Ibid., p. 275. [6]

Chronicles, Chambers, ed., pp. 136–137. [7]

Quarles, *The Negro in the Making of America,* p. 132. [8]

Franklin, *Slavery to Freedom,* pp. 325–326. [9]

Logan, *The Betrayal,* p. 25. [10]

Franklin, *Slavery to Freedom,* pp. 332–333. [11]

Logan, *The Betrayal,* pp. 97–98. [12]

Franklin, *Slavery to Freedom,* p. 431. [13]

Ibid., p. 432. [14]

Ibid., p. 432. [15]

Eric Lincoln, *Negro Pilgrimage* (New York, Bantam, 1967), p. 81. [16]

Franklin, *Slavery to Freedom,* pp. 432–433. [17]

Ibid., p. 435. [18]

Ibid., pp. 435–436. [19]

Ibid., p. 467. [20]

Quarles, *The Negro in the Making of America,* p. 187. [21]

Franklin, *Slavery to Freedom,* p. 467. [22]

Ibid., p. 472. **23**

Ibid., p. 474. See also *Black Protest,* Grant, ed., pp. **24**
187–191.

Franklin, *Slavery to Freedom,* pp. 475–476. **25**

Ibid., p. 581. **26**

Ibid., p. 241. **27**

Quarles, *The Negro in the Making of America,* p. 241. **28**

See Ida Wells-Barnett, *On Lynchings* (New York, Arna **29**
Press and *The New York Times,* 1969).

Selected Poems of Claude McKay. **30**

9
back to
africa

Black soldiers returned from the European war in 1918 only to find an American war going on. They had fought to "make the world safe for Democracy,"[1] and now this same democratic system turned on the very men who had fought to protect it. The revived Ku Klux Klan achieved a membership of five million, and a wave of anti-black hatred swept the country. The summer of 1919, called "The Red Summer" by writer James Weldon Johnson,[2] saw twenty-five race riots in American cities directed against black citizens. Black soldiers returned to this situation, and America did not welcome them as heroes. The historian John Hope Franklin presents the harsh facts:

> White citizens, in and out of the Klan, poured out a wrath upon the Negro population shortly after the war that could hardly be viewed as fit punishment even for a treasonable group of persons. More than 70 Negroes were lynched during the first year of the post-war period. Ten Negro soldiers, several still in their uniforms, were lynched. Mississippi and Georgia mobs murdered three returned soldiers each; in Arkansas two were lynched; while

Florida and Alabama each took the life of a Negro soldier by mob violence. Fourteen Negroes were burned publicly, eleven of whom were burned alive. In utter despair a Negro editor of Charleston, South Carolina, cried out, "There is scarcely a day that passes that newspapers don't tell about a Negro soldier lynched in his uniform."[3]

A Leader Emerges

White America was a dismal place for its black population. It seemed that the black man could do nothing to please the white majority. Centuries of slave labor, receiving leftovers from the American economy, even fighting America's wars could not stop America from hating its black citizens. Ironically, these same citizens realized that the black soldiers who died defending this country would not even be allowed to vote in many states.

Progress had been made, it is true. Organizations like the NAACP were working towards securing justice, especially in the courts. But progress was slow. And such organizations never reached the mass of black people. Their membership lists were comparatively small. In fact, many black men in America viewed the NAACP as an upper class club of both black and white members. And although DuBois became the leading black spokesman since the death of Washington in 1915, he did not make his appeal to the masses. His interest lay in the "talented tenth."[4] The ordinary black citizen, *disenfranchised* in the South, and *ghettoized* in the north did not see many signs of progress. American society had separated itself from its black citizens. Into this dismal scene walked Marcus Mosiah Garvey. He strutted, lectured, and changed the face of American black society.

We are too large and great in numbers not to be a great people, a great race, and a great nation. We are the descendants of a suffering people. We are the descendants of a people determined to suffer no longer. The time has now come when we must seek our place in the sun.[5]

The hour has come for the Negro to take his own initiative. No more fear, no more cringing, no more sycophantic begging and pleading. Destiny leads us to liberty, to freedom; that freedom that Victoria of England never gave; that liberty that Lincoln never meant; that freedom, that liberty, that will see us men among men, that will make us a great and powerful people.[6]

The man who spoke this emotional call came originally from Jamaica.[7] In 1916 he arrived in New York, settled in Harlem, and went about setting up a chapter of his organization—"The Universal Negro Improvement Association" (UNIA). No other leader in America had ever attracted to himself masses of black followers. In five years Garvey had done just that. In any judgment, it was a remarkable feat. Men listened to his message because it was a necessary one for that time. Garvey told his audiences that blackness of skin was not a matter of shame, as this country thought, but one of pride. Moreover, he said black was the most beautiful color. That Africa was a great land with great civilizations. This formed the essential core of Garvey's message to America's black people.[8] The one word which sums it up is *pride*.

Besides extolling Africa, he declared that it had to be free, instead of being governed by white foreigners. He even formed the *Universal African Legion,* to fight a war of liberation; in 1921 he declared himself "Provisional President" of free Africa.[9] Such interest and pride in the homeland, although rather fantastic, spoke a new message to America's black population, many of whom thought Africa the land of savages.

> We declare to the world that Africa must be free, that the entire Negro race must be emancipated from industrial bondage, peonage and serfdom; we make no compromise, we make no apology in this our declaration. We do not desire to create offense on the part of other races, but we are determined that we shall be heard, that we shall be given the rights to which we are entitled.[10]

And so, Garvey launched his "Back to Africa" movement. Although the program never succeeded in getting many people to go to Africa, it signaled a psychological shift in attitude. The black American was redeveloping roots that went back further than slavery.

In Garvey's program religion changed colors. In his African Orthodox Church, angels were black and devils were white. The "Black Man of Sorrows"[11] and the "Black Virgin Mother"[12] were worshipped.

Garvey did not direct his interest to the "talented tenth."[13] He spoke to the man in the streets. And he liked these men to be as black as possible. The blacker the better, because that signified "pure blood," unmixed with that of the white man.[14] In this he reversed the situation of the black-mulatto question. Traditionally, because of white opinion, a lighter skin was held in esteem in the Negro community; lighter skin signified a higher status. But now Garvey challenged that, placing the blackest of skin in first place. The "talented tenth," most of whom had light skin, did not favor

Garvey's special brand of racism. However, even this helped bolster the spirits of the black community in this crucial time.

Unlike the NAACP, Marcus Mosiah Garvey closed membership in his UNIA to white men. Moreover, he refused any financial help from the white community. He wanted his projects totally accomplished by black men. In fact, he and his paper *The Negro World* criticized the NAACP for encouraging integration. He accused the organization of favoring light-colored skins—even of being more white than black. And he dubbed it "The National Association for the Advancement of *(certain)* Colored People."[15] In a speech given in 1922, he carefully distinguished the UNIA from other groups:

> The difference between the Universal Negro Improvement Association and the other movements of this country, and probably the world, is that the Universal Negro Improvement Association seeks independence of government, while the other organizations seek to make the Negro a secondary part of existing governments.[16]

Rise and Fall

The astounding rise of Garvey did not come about just by his charismatic personality and the urgency of his message. The new, urban situation of the black community helped it. For a decade or more, black population began to shift from the rural South to the urban North. So, great populations of black Americans were concentrated in one place. A black leader in America, for the first time, addressed himself to a great audience of black people.

In 1921, Garvey seemed at the height of his

power. In the UNIA convention that year, he led 50,000 followers through the streets of New York. Flags, bands, and Garvey himself in a resplendent uniform led the way to a mass rally in Madison Square Garden. In the past two years, he claimed, contributions had amounted to ten million dollars. This backing enabled him to put some of his grand ideas into effect, but led eventually to his downfall just a few years later.

His most famous enterprise was the *Black Star Line*—three ships[17] he bought in order to transport select black Americans to Africa. There, they would work towards African freedom and make the continent a homeland for the world's black people.

Yet, in just two years the *Black Star Line* was bankrupt, and Garvey was accused of "Using the Mails to Defraud."[18] Even a critic like DuBois admitted the basic honesty of Garvey. But Garvey surrounded himself with incompetent advisors. DuBois said: "When it comes to Mr. Garvey's industrial and commercial enterprises, there is more ground for doubt and misgiving than in the matter of his character."[19] Nevertheless, in 1925, Garvey went to prison;[20] two years later President Harding gave him a pardon, but sent him back to Jamaica. Garvey never returned to the U.S. He died in England in 1940. But his message was not forgotten in this country. It had a great effect on subsequent ideas.

DuBois Challenged

Garvey challenged the Negro intellectuals of his day, especially DuBois. In general, he accused them of being an 'aristocracy"[21] neglecting the black masses and of identifying with white culture rather than with Negro culture. He said they were not black enough, and gave as an example their neglect of Africa. The majority of Negro leaders, in turn, rejected him because of his unsound business enterprises and his pompous titles like "Provisional President of Africa"[22] and

"Knights of the Distinguished Order of Ethiopia."[23] Despite their opposition, Garvey assembled a following of at least a half-million followers, and many more millions who were sympathetic to his message. The black man in America needed the message of pride in blackness and hope for the future of which Garvey spoke.

> We shall march out, yes, as black American citizens, as black British subjects, as black French citizens, as black Italians or as black Spaniards, but we shall march out with a greater loyalty, the loyalty of race. We shall march out in answer to the cry of our fathers, who cry out to us for the redemption of our own country, our motherland, Africa. . . .[24]

Sober voices like DuBois' were right in criticizing Garvey's unsound business sense, and his preference for blackness which amounted to inverse racism. Yet, he gave something to the black citizens of this country. He gave them a message of *emotion*—a passionate belief in the beauty and strength of black-skinned people, a new love for African ancestry, and a sense of power in the united convictions of black men.

Nor did Garvey's message limit itself to America. His voice was loud in demanding African independence. In that he was prophetic, although he died before seeing his dream come true. Kwame Nkrumah, the first President of Ghana, in writing about his studies in the United States said: "Of all the literature I studied, the book that did more than any other to fire my opinion was *The Philosophy and Opinions of Marcus Garvey*."[25]

Garvey's career, then, lasted only briefly. But in those few years he colorfully took up the banner of the black masses, opposed leading intellectuals like DuBois, and planted pride in people *because they were black,* not because they were trying to be whites. One expert makes this judgment on the Garvey era: "The inner shame over blackness was by no means exorcised, but after Garvey it was never again quite the same as it had been."[26]

footnotes

Quarles, *The Negro in the Making of America,* p. 190.   **1**

Franklin, *Slavery to Freedom,* pp. 472–473.   **2**

Ibid., p. 472.   **3**

Rudwick, *W.E.B. DuBois,* p. 104.   **4**

A composite speech of Marcus Garvey, from Martin   **5**
Dubermann's play *In White America* (New York, Signet, 1965), p. 68.

Ibid., p. 69.   **6**

Quarles, *The Negro in the Making of America,* pp. 195–   **7**
197. Also, Hughes and Meltzer, *Pictorial History,* pp. 270–271.

Black Protest, Grant, ed., p. 202   **8**

Franklin, *Slavery to Freedom,* p. 482.   **9**

Black Protest, Grant, ed., p. 200   **10**

Quarles, *The Negro in the Making of America,* p. 196.   **11**

Ibid., p. 196.   **12**

For the break between DuBois and Garvey, see Rud-   **13**
wick, *W.E.B. DuBois,* p. 216 ff.

Ibid., pp. 229–230.   **14**

Ibid., p. 228.   **15**

Chronicles, Chambers, ed., p. 218.   **16**

Franklin, *Slavery to Freedom,* pp. 482–483.   **17**

Ibid., p. 483.   **18**

Rudwick, *W.E.B. DuBois,* p. 217.   **19**

Franklin, *Slavery to Freedom,* p. 483.   **20**

Rudwick, *W.E.B. DuBois,* pp. 218–219. **21**

Franklin, *Slavery to Freedom,* p. 482. **22**

Ibid., p. 482. **23**

Chronicles, Chambers, ed., p. 220. **24**

Silberman, *Crisis,* p. 147. **25**

Harold Jacobs, quoted in Silberman's *Crisis,* p. 137. **26**

10
black
pilgrimage

I'm telling it like it *is!* You *never* have to worry about me biting my tongue if something I know as truth is on my mind. Raw, naked truth exchanged between the black man and white man is what a whole lot more of is needed in this country—to clear the air of the racial mirages, clichés, and lies that this country's very atmosphere has been filled with for four hundred years.[1]

The man who spoke these words became a symbol for the black revolution. He was a hero to many of the 22,000,000 African-Americans in this country. He was a threat to what he called the "white establishment" who feared words like violence, nationalism, separatism, and revolution. In the eyes of many he died a martyr to his cause when he was murdered during a speech he was giving on February 21, 1965.[2]

The life of Malcolm Little[3] had many acts, and taken as a whole he easily becomes one of the most dramatic personalities in mid-twentieth century history. His early life gave little indication of the international fame he was to achieve. At Omaha in 1925 he was born into violence. One of his uncles had been lynched, and two others had been killed by white men. Another uncle was later shot by policemen, and Malcolm's own father was to meet death violently. The family of Reverend Earl Little, a Baptist minister, was forced to move from Omaha to Milwaukee to East Lansing, and finally, to a small farm outside that city.[4]

Malcolm's father was not a popular man with the white community. He was a militant follower of Marcus Garvey. The movement Garvey led in the early 1920s, the UNIA, preached black pride, even supremacy, over white America. Although Garvey's call back to Africa produced few concrete results, the spirit of nationalistic pride and self-help made a deep impression on his millions of followers, and the generation which followed them. Rev. Little's involvement in this movement—independence from the white man—was the reason for the constant persecution of his family, the frequent moves, the burning down of his home, and of his brutal murder when Malcolm was six years old. Malcolm found out early that he had to fight if he were to survive. Unfortunately, the odds were stacked against him. The depression years offered few possibilities for his mother, Louise, to support six children, especially since his father had made so many enemies among the white establishment. Not only her race, but her name was held against her. Finally the family accepted welfare. Malcolm's memories are not pleasant ones:

> When the State Welfare people began coming to our house, we would come from school sometimes and find them talking with our mother, asking a thousand questions, they acted and looked at her and at us, and around in our house in a way that had about it the feeling—at least for me—that we were not people. In their eyesight

we were just *things,* that was all. . . . they acted as if they owned us.[5]

Pressures from all sides became too great for Malcolm's mother. Society took away her husband, her pride, and finally, her family.[6] We can hardly wonder that Malcolm had little praise for the American social structures:

the white man wins all the time. He's a professional gambler; he has all the cards and the odds stacked on his side, and he has always dealt to our people from the bottom of the deck. . . . Hence I have no mercy or compassion in me for a society that will crush people, and then penalize them for not being able to stand up under the weight.[7]

Malcolm became a ward of the state. He called it "legal, modern slavery."[8] A foster home, trouble at school, and expulsion followed in quick order, until the thirteen-year-old boy found himself in reform school. For a brief time, some of Malcolm's natural traits came out, those same qualities which would later mark him as a leader of men—intelligence, popularity, and ambition. His return to school proved successful. His work stood out, and his fellow students even elected him as their class president. Hopes and ambitions for the future rose. One day he told his teacher his ambition in life was to become a lawyer. His teacher looked surprised and then answered him.

Malcolm, one of life's first needs is for us to be realistic. Don't misunderstand me, now. We all like you, you know that. But you've got to be realistic about being a nigger. A lawyer—that's no realistic goal

for a nigger. You need to think about something you *can* be.[9]

Malcolm understood that teacher well: whites
can have ambitions, "niggers" can't. In the keen mind
of the teen-ager, an image and judgment of what American society offered him was forming. The "Brass Spit-
toons" by Langston Hughes makes this picture clear:

> Clean the spittoon, boy.
> > Detroit,
> > Chicago,
> > Atlantic City,
> > Palm Beach.
>
> Clean the spittoons.
> The steam in hotel kitchens,
> And the smoke in hotel lobbies,
> And the slime in hotel spittoons:
> Part of my life.
>
> > Hey, boy!
> > A nickel,
> > A dime,
> > A dollar,
> Two dollars a day.
>
> > Hey, boy!
> > A nickel,
> > A dime,
> > A dollar,
> Two dollars . . .[10]

Even in the detention home, where Mr. and Mrs.
Swerlin treated him with kindness, Malcolm detected
false love. They regarded him as a kind of house pet,
or mascot, rather than another person. "They would

talk about anything and everything with me standing right there hearing them, the same way people would talk freely in front of a pet canary."[11]

He was a nigger in school, with a "realistic future" ahead of him, and a house pet at home. Strangely enough, Malcolm had no anger within him at this time. He couldn't afford it. He lived in a white man's world, and he had to fit himself into the slots they carved out for him even if these spelled "nigger" and "boy." He was trying very hard, in those days, in every possible way, to be "white." Then, suddenly, came the meeting that changed his life, the visit of his sister Ella.

A Beautiful Woman

His past experiences worked hard towards making Malcolm try to fit into white America; his miseducation was almost completely geared to make him ashamed of his own race. His history book contained one paragraph on the history of Negroes; his teacher added that they "were usually lazy and dumb and shiftless."[12] Ella began to change that false image for her half brother. She had a different self-concept than the one *taught* to Malcolm: "she was the first, really proud black woman I had ever seen in my life. She was plainly proud of her very dark skin. This was unheard of among Negroes in those days."[13]

That summer Ella invited her brother to spend the vacation with her in Boston. Malcolm went to that city, and a new world opened up to him, a much larger, more exciting world. And for the first time, Malcolm came into close contact with black culture. The white world did not die in him yet; that would take many more years. But its obituary was in prospect. He no longer felt comfortable in the roles of "nigger," "boy," and "mascot." After coming into contact with the city, learning that black people had size, culture, and pride, he

95

could never again feel comfortable in his old roles. At the end of the school term, Malcolm left Lansing and went to Boston to live with Ella.

False Heroes

A new kind of education began in Boston. Step by step, Malcolm learned the ladder that leads down to tragedy. How did this happen? He possessed leadership abilities, high intelligence, and ambition. Yet, in just six years, even before he turned twenty-one, his criminal record included dope peddling, the numbers racket, pimping, and armed robbery.

> "Count one, eight to ten years—
> "Count two, eight to ten years—
> "Count three . . .
> "The sentences to run concurrently."[14]

This, for a young man who only a few years previously had wanted to become a lawyer!

Men with drive and talents like Malcolm rise or fight themselves to the top of their society. Rejected in fact by American society as a "nigger," Malcolm gradually came to rise to the top of another society— the underworld. An urban ghetto, where poverty, frustration, alienation, and the lack of privacy drive men to seek any outlet possible, presents a fine breeding place for crime. Later, Malcolm described such conditions as "spiritually, economically, and politically sick."[15]

His heroes became the man with money, with flashy clothes, cool talk, and physical toughness. Who else could he look up to? The men who murdered his father? The teacher who taught "Negro history" in one paragraph and said niggers were dumb, lazy, and shiftless? The people who treated him "kindly" as a house pet? Malcolm's range of possibilities narrowed.

He saw money, clothes, girls, liquor, and dope, and he took the steps necessary to have these. In just a few years he became, not a famous lawyer, but a famous criminal. White America did not offer Malcolm many heroes to imitate.

Prison Education

> Bimbi was the first Negro convict I'd known who didn't respond to "What'cha know, Daddy?" Often, after we had done our day's license quota, we would sit around, perhaps 15 of us, and listen to Bimbi. Normally, white prisoners wouldn't think of listening to Negro prisoners' opinions on anything, but guards, even, would wander over close to hear Bimbi on any subject. He would have a cluster of people riveted. . . .[16]

Bimbi was a new hero, one who spoke intelligently, could argue persuasively, and had gotten knowledge from books (that great strength that counts, in the end, more than mere muscle-power). Malcolm recognized this and at Bimbi's encouragement began serious study again. As with everything he ever did, Malcolm plunged wholeheartedly into this task he set for himself. He copied dictionaries to learn the meaning of words, he read far into the night, studying sometimes 15 hours a day. He learned philosophy, poetry, and history, especially African-American history. "I don't think anybody ever got more out of prison than I did,"[17] he later commented.

In later years, interviewers of Malcolm expressed astonishment at the range of his knowledge, the depth of his intelligence, and the clarity of his answers. He was no man's fool, and he was called perhaps the angriest man in America.

Can we wonder why he was angry? Born into violence, a nightmare of a childhood, father murdered, home broken up, educated to despise his own heritage, and ambitions frustrated, what choices remained for Malcolm Little except to be a white man's lackey or a ghetto inhabitant? And yet this man had great talents which might have been totally lost (as so many countless others are lost), had it not been for two heroes he discovered in prison: Bimbi, who opened to him the world of knowledge; and the Honorable Elijah Muhammad,[18] who opened to him the world of religion.

footnotes

The Autobiography of Malcolm X, p. 273.   **1**

Ibid., pp. 434–436, described by Alex Haley. Eldridge   **2** Cleaver, in *Soul on Ice,* tells about various reactions to Malcolm's assassination, pp. 50–61.

Malcolm X, *Autobiography,* p. 1. Malcolm's original fam-   **3** ily name. The "X" was given to him when he was received into the Nation of Islam, *Autobiography,* p. 199.

Ibid., pp. 2–3.   **4**

Ibid., p. 12.   **5**

Ibid., p. 16.   **6**

Ibid., p. 22.   **7**

Ibid., p. 21.   **8**

Ibid., p. 36.   **9**

Hughes, *Fine Clothes to the Jew* (New York, Knopf,   **10** 1927).

Autobiography, p. 26.   **11**

Ibid., p. 29.   **12**

Ibid., p. 32.   **13**

Ibid., p. 151.   **14**

Ibid., p. 218. Also, p. 313. **15**

Ibid., p. 153. **16**

Ibid., p. 180. **17**

Malcolm describes his initial contact with the Honorable **18**
Elijah Muhammad in the *Autobiography,* p. 155 ff.

11
malcolm x

The Muslims "X" symbolized the true African family name that he never could know. For me, my "X" replaced the white slave-master name of "Little" which some blue-eyed devil named Little had imposed on my paternal forebears.[1]

With the enthusiasm and determination which characterized everything he did—whether selling sandwiches, pushing dope, or reading books—Malcolm embraced religion as taught by the Honorable Elijah Muhammad, leader of the Muslim movement in America. The origins and present program of the "Black Muslims"[2] appear in Chapter 12.

Malcolm's family introduced him to the teaching of Mr. Muhammad in 1948. Between this time and 1952, when Malcolm was released from prison, he converted completely to the religion of Islam as taught by Mr. Muhammad. This was no easy task; it demanded that Malcolm give up smoking, liquor, narcotics, cigarettes, and pork. Moreover, he had to dedicate himself to the rigid standards of moral conduct required by the Muslim code. Most important of all, however, Malcolm re-

nounced the atheism he had professed, and acknowl-
edged his belief in the one God of Islam—Allah.

Religious conviction came at an important time
in Malcolm's life. His descent into crime, drugs, theft,
and depersonalized sex emptied his soul of all values
except survival. Now, the emptiness within him began
to fill. Bimbi showed him how to learn; the teachings of
Muhammad showed him how to live. Malcolm's life took
on new shape and meaning. He left prison a changed
man. Discipline, religion, education, and intense anger
against white Christian America prepared him for the
kind of crusade he was to wage:

> Christianity is the white man's religion. The
> Holy Bible in the white man's hands and
> his interpretations of it have been the
> greatest single ideological weapon for en-
> slaving millions of non-white human
> beings. Every country the white man has
> conquered with his guns, he has always
> paved the way, and salved his conscience,
> by carrying the Bible and interpreting it to
> call the people 'heathens' and 'pagans';
> then he sends his guns, then his mission-
> aries behind the guns to mop up. . . .[3]

With anger like this within him, Malcolm joined
his family in Detroit, and immediately he began to work
for the Nation of Islam. After a meeting with Mr. Muhammad, who had written to him in prison, Malcolm
began actively seeking converts to Islam, which brought
him from Detroit to Boston, Philadelphia, and finally
New York. He left few possibilities of recruiting unexplored: pool halls, bars, street corners—all these saw
the presence of Malcolm X exhorting men and women
to submit to the teachings of Elijah Muhammad. One
of his favorite places to win converts turned out to be
Christian churches, after their Sunday service:

Brothers and sisters, the white man has brainwashed us black people to fasten our gaze upon a blond-haired, blue-eyed Jesus! We're worshipping a Jesus that doesn't even *look* like us! Oh, yes! Now just bear with me, listen to the teachings of the Messenger of Allah, the Honorable Elijah Muhammad. Now, just think of this. The blond-haired, blue-eyed white man has taught you and me to worship a *white* Jesus, and shout and sing and pray until we *die,* to wait until *death,* for some dreamy heaven-in-the-hereafter, when we're *dead* while this white man has his milk and honey in the streets paved with golden dollars right here on *this* earth![4]

Malcolm crisscrossed America like St. Paul journeyed through the Roman world. The gospel of Malcolm, however, was hatred for the "white devils"[5] who had oppressed the black man in America for four hundred years. His energy, his speaking ability, bluntness, and eventual capture of the mass media went far in building up the numbers and strength of the Nation of Islam in those years. Malcolm's style shocked people whether they heard him on television, read about him in magazines, or listened to him in a lecture hall. Sometimes his hatred took on extreme forms, as the time he publicly rejoiced because a plane with one hundred and twenty whites crashed—calling it "a beautiful thing that has happened."[6]

Despite his constantly professed loyalty to Elijah Muhammad, tensions arose between the two men. Malcolm blamed this on the jealousy of rivals, the hesitation of the Nation of Islam in adopting his activist programs, and lacks in the character of Mr. Muhammad himself. A break late in 1963, after Malcolm made imprudent public statements about the assassination of President John Kennedy, Mr. Muhammad silenced Malcolm for ninety days.[7] At first, he accepted the punishment, but gradually realized it might have far greater effects than a mere temporary loss of his public voice. A spiritual crisis long in the making broke out. Malcolm made his decision to separate himself from the movement he had worked in for a dozen years, and to set up a new organization—the *Organization of Afro-American Unity* (OAU) came into existence, "a non-religious and non-sectarian group organized to unite Afro-Americans for a constructive program toward attainment of human rights."[8]

Pilgrimage to Mecca

Perhaps because of the spiritual crisis he had undergone, Malcolm chose at this time to fulfill one of the most important religious duties the Islamic religion requires—the journey to Mecca, the Muslims' holy city.[9] He had broken with the "Black Muslims" and now felt the need to strengthen his ties with the more orthodox roots of the Moslem religion. Difficulties arose because Moslems in this country do not admit that followers of Elijah Muhammad are orthodox believers.[10] Through the aid of friends, however, and by his own obvious sincerity, Malcolm was permitted to enter the city of Mecca open only to orthodox Moslems, and thus make the Hajj—the holy pilgrimage. Malcolm strengthened himself religiously:

> My feeling there in the House of God was a numbness. My *Mutaivaf* (guide) led me in the crowd of praying, chanting pilgrims, moving seven times around the Ka'ba. Some were bent and wizened with age; it was a sight that stamped itself on the

brain. I saw incapacitated pilgrims being carried by others. Faces were enraptured in their faith. The seventh time around, I prayed two *Rak'a,* prostrating myself, my head on the floor. The first prostration, I prayed the Quran verse "Say He is God, the one and only. . . ."[11]

Besides going back to his spiritual roots, Malcolm took this opportunity to make contact with his ethnic roots also, and toured several countries in Africa. He was received with great honor everywhere he went, given lavish hospitality, and asked to speak before audiences interested in the struggle he had dedicated himself to. Nigerians gave him a new name in the Yoruba language—Omowale, "the son who has come home."[12] A new idea occurred to him when he saw how the emerging nations of Africa were working to loosen themselves from oppression: that the struggle of the black man is international. His next move—causing a sensation in this country—suggested bringing the question of African-Americans before the United Nations! This whole line of thinking shows how Malcolm discovered unity between himself, the Moslem world, and African nations. He joined his fight to Pan-Africanism.

Back to America

Many Moslems must wait until they near the end of their life to fulfill the *Hajj.* Malcolm, unwittingly, did the same, although he was only in his late thirties. He returned to this country with too many enemies. Not only did he attack the white man now, but also the black man—the Muslims. On February 21, 1965, only thirty-nine years old, he was assassinated while giving a speech.[13] He was born into violence, and he died by violence.

Change in Attitude

During the last part of his life, Malcolm's attitude towards white America changed. The earlier hatred of all the white "devils"[14] became more selective. Two causes brought this about. First of all, the constant invitations he received from white campuses and the attentive audiences he spoke to there made him realize that many young people in America felt themselves joined to the cause of African-Americans. "The young whites, and blacks too, are the only hope America has," he said. "The rest of us have always been living a lie."[15] The experience of the *Hajj* was the second reason for his change in attitude. On that pilgrimage to Mecca he knew and felt fraternities with many men. "The *brotherhood!*" he exclaimed. "The people of all races, colors, from all over the world coming together as *one!* It has proved to me the power of the One God."[16] Malcolm himself publicly admitted his change in attitude:

> In the past, yes. I have made sweeping indictments of all white people. I never will be guilty of that again—as I know now that some white people *are* truly sincere, that some truly are capable of being brotherly toward a black man. The true Islam has shown me that a blanket indictment of all white people is as wrong as when whites make blanket indictments against blacks.[17]

Eldridge Cleaver, a black leader and author, calls Malcolm a "martyr." Cleaver, in San Quentin prison at the time of the assassination, was a Muslim who chose to follow Malcolm instead of Elijah Muhammad. He speaks of Malcolm's transformation after the *Hajj:* "Malcolm X, in the eyes of Elijah's followers, had committed the unforgivable heresy when, changing his views and abandoning the racist position, he admitted the possibility of brotherhood between blacks and whites."[18] Cleaver speaks of many Muslims "who were glad to be liberated from a doctrine of hate and racial supremacy."[19]

The Meaning of Malcolm X

The meaning of Malcolm X is clear; he must not be repeated. His life shows us what can happen to a man who is born into a society of violence and hatred. His religious awakening, his dedication to a cause, his brutal honesty, and his martyrdom challenge every American today to change this society of violence and racial hatred. There is no other way to go, except toward ever increasing violence which makes the rest of the world look at us with increasing suspicion, and makes even thoughtful men wonder if our society is truly walking towards destruction. Malcolm, the kid from the ghetto, the dope pusher, thief, convict, religious leader, the honest man speaks this challenge. He speaks, above all, as a black American:

> But as racism leads America up the suicide path, I do believe, from the experiences that I have had with them, that the whites of the younger generation, in the colleges and universities, will see the handwriting on the wall and many of them will turn to the *spiritual* path of *truth*—the *only* way left to America to ward off the disaster that racism inevitably must lead to.[20]

footnotes

Malcolm X, *Autobiography,* p. 199. For the changing of   1
the name in the Nation of Islam, see C. Eric Lincoln,

The Black Muslims in America (Boston, Beacon, 1961), pp. 109–110.

The Nation of Islam is the official name of the movement headed by the Honorable Elijah Muhammad. [2]

Malcolm X, *Autobiography,* p. 241. [3]

Ibid., p. 220. [4]

Ibid., p. 207. [5]

Ibid., p. 394. Also, Silberman, *Crisis,* p. 56. [6]

Ibid., pp. 300–302. [7]

Ibid., p. 416. [8]

The pilgrimage to Mecca is a religious duty which devout Moslems try to fulfill at least once in their lifetime. It is encouraged by the Nation of Islam. See Lincoln, *Black Muslims,* p. 219. [9]

Malcolm X., *Autobiography,* p. 348. This attitude, however, seems to be gradually changing. See Lincoln, "The Black Muslims and Orthodox Islam," in *Black Muslims,* pp. 210–226. Mr. Lincoln says on p. 212 that, "There seems good reason to believe that the Black Muslims will soon be officially sheltered in the community of international Islam." Significant also, is the fact that the Honorable Elijah Muhammad made the pilgrimage to Mecca, which is accessible only to Moslem believers. See Eric Lincoln, *Black Muslims,* p. 226. [10]

Malcolm X, *Autobiography,* p. 337. [11]

Ibid., p. 351. [12]

Described by Alex Haley in the Epilogue to Malcolm's *Autobiography,* pp. 434–435. [13]

Ibid., p. 266. [14]

Ibid., p. 400. [15]

Ibid., p. 338. [16]

Ibid., p. 362. [17]

Eldridge Cleaver, *Soul on Ice* (New York: McGraw-Hill, **18** 1968), p. 56.

Ibid., p. 56. **19**

Malcolm X, *Autobiography,* p. 341. **20**

12
the black
muslims

"The Hate That Hate Produced" showed white America, in 1959, what centuries of racism in this country gave birth to—black hatred. From their television screens, Americans learned about the Nation of Islam,[1] whose members despise United States citizenship, train a select private army, declare that the white man is in reality the devil, and demand a portion of this country in which to establish a separate, black nation, totally independent of the United States. Comfortable people were shocked. Yet, when considered, the Black Muslim[2] philosophy simply reverses the usual American pattern. In place of white racism, it teaches black racism; it carries the ghetto—produced by white men—to a logical development. This country has enslaved black men and treated them as second class citizens, so why should they value citizenship? The strength and appeal of the Muslim way of life has produced a huge wave of conversions—by 1961 sixty-nine temples ministered to Muslims in twenty-seven states. Membership lists are kept secret, but estimates range from 100,000 to 200,000 believers.

Origins

The movement began in 1930,[3] the depression era, when even white men had trouble finding jobs. A supposed traveling salesman, W. D. Fard[4] walked into the troubled black community of Detroit. He announced that he came from the holy city of Mecca and that he carried the true message of history and the way of salvation for all black men and women.[5] For the next four years Fard's audience grew, and his followers listened intently to his words. He chose Elijah Poole as his chief disciple, giving him the name of Elijah Muhammad. After Poole's mysterious disappearance in 1934, Elijah Muhammad took over the leadership of the Temple of Islam. He declared then that he believed W. D. Fard was actually Allah; Muhammad himself was the "Messenger of Allah."[6] Troubled times came and some questioned Muhammad's leadership. Nevertheless, new temples, later called "mosques," arose in Chicago, Washington, and Milwaukee. In 1942, however, Elijah Muhammad, convicted of, among other things, counseling young men to avoid the draft, went to prison until 1946.[7]

The 1950s saw an astounding rise in Black Muslim membership. Part of this must be attributed to the dynamism of Malcolm X, Muhammad's "First National Minister," who later broke away from the movement. The growth is all the more surprising when we consider the extremely strict moral code of the Muslims. They forbid the eating of pork, and several other "unclean" foods, and they allow no alcoholic drink, tobacco, or narcotics. The Muslims reject Christianity as the "white man's religion."[8] They accept the Koran and the Bible as Holy Books, but they say the latter has been misinterpreted. The Muslims even give a unique view of history, contending that the white man is the product of centuries of misbreeding.

Black Muslim Mythology

Among the original black men of the earth, who founded the holy city of Mecca, Mr. Yakub, a scientist, caused trouble. This took place about 4500 B.C. Authorities in Mecca finally had to exile him and his followers—59,999 of them—to the island of Patmos. Out of revenge, Yakub decided to breed a "devil race" of men—the white men. Although he died when he was one hundred fifty-two years old, his successors followed out his mad plan which took eight hundred years to accomplish. Finally they made their way back to the mainland, among the original black people—the "natural" men. It was soon learned that this "devil race" specialized in making trouble; the black men exiled them, sending them off to Europe, where they lived lives little better than animals. However, prophecy said this white race would eventually rule the world, but would be superseded once more by the black race. One especially strong tribe of black men—Shabazz— were to be brought to North America. As slaves there they would learn the duplicity and evil of the white man. In our own times, the transfer of power from the white devil race to the black original race is to take place.[9]

The Muslim Program

Besides a radically different view of history, the Muslims offer clear-cut political and social demands. Among other things, they want a separate, independent nation set up for black men:

> Since we cannot get along with them in peace and equality after giving them 400 years of our sweat and blood and receiving in return some of the worst treatment human beings have ever experienced, we believe our contributions to this land, and the sufferings forced on us by white America, justifies our demand for complete separation in a state or territory of our own.[10]

The Muslims also call for freedom for black prisoners; a black educational program; exemption from taxation; an end to mob attacks, police brutality, and wars which give them nothing to gain. They also believe intermarriage between races should be forbidden.

Besides the political and religious structures, Muslims offer their members a thriving social life around mosque-centered activities. The men can join the "fruit of Islam," a kind of private army within the Nation, the women learn household skills, and the youth study the teachings of Muhammad.

No one doubts that in its own way the Muslim program has accomplished much good. *The New York Times Magazine* has said this of Muhammad: "Alone of all the Negro leaders, Elijah Muhammad has a vivid awareness of the vital need of a new birth." Muhammad insists that his followers cultivate racial consciousness—pride in being black. Stability comes into families which organize themselves around a strict line of ritual and authority. The Muslims point out with pride that there is almost no problem of crime or juvenile delinquency among the "brothers and sisters." Even secular agencies marvel at the Muslims' success in treating ex-convicts and former dope addicts. In the Temple of Islam, these men find themselves honored, helped, and put on a new path of life. The philosophy of Elijah Muhammad stresses self-help—the black man must free himself from dependence on white culture. Muslims work at establishing their own businesses, patronizing these, thus putting back into the black community the money it so sorely needs. Finally, Elijah Muhammad has been, for many, a source of black unity, pride, and dramatic protest against the "children of the slave masters." He clearly stands out as a charismatic leader of strength and importance.

Muslim Weaknesses

The strongest—and at the same time—the weakest point of Muslim teaching is that they have ruled out the possibility of brotherhood with the white man. This automatically narrows their future in American society to several possibilities: first, they can continue as a small but vocal protest group; second, they can actually see their dreams of a separate state realized; third, they can change their philosophy to admit that perhaps white and black men can live together in peace, justice, and equality. Many would question whether a black racist philosophy is the effective answer to the white racist policy which has dominated our country. Thinking men, both black and white, still dream of a truly united country. Malcolm X, the most devoted of Elijah's followers, eventually came to this conclusion after his numerous contacts with college students, and his pilgrimage to Mecca:

> I have eaten from the same plate with people whose eyes were the bluest of blue, whose hair was the blondest of blond and whose skin was the whitest of white . . . and I felt the sincerity in the words and deeds of these "white" Muslims that I felt among the African Muslims of Nigeria, Sudan, and Ghana.[11]

Eldridge Cleaver, another black leader and writer, says that Malcolm's disagreement with the philosophy of the Muslims liberated him "from a doctrine of hate and racial supremacy."[12] Because of the defection of Malcolm and others like him the Muslims are no longer as united as they once were.

The Effect of the Muslims

An article appearing in the Muslim newspaper *Muhammad Speaks* accused black leaders throughout the country of taking Elijah Muhammad's ideas, yet failing to give him credit for these:

> The above mentioned Black men and others have literally "stolen" portions of the

> Honorable Elijah Muhammad's Message
> to the Black Man in America. . . . The
> Black men who speak of what must be
> done to clean up the ghettos are only
> quoting what the Messenger of Allah has
> said. . . . Even the term "Black Power"
> was stolen from our Divine Leader and
> Teacher. He has been teaching separation
> and Black Power for thirty-eight years.[13]

There is no doubt that the ideas expressed by Elijah Muhammad have influenced much thinking within the black community. When Jim White, a Chicago teen-ager says, "Pride, that's it. I guess you gotta have your pride, no matter what. If you don't have pride, you're pretty lost,"[14] he echoes feelings that the Muslim movement preached for years. Mr. Muhammad constantly stresses the need for unity among black men; black power grows out from this idea naturally. And in his idea of a separate territory governed by blacks, even this has achieved serious discussion recently. The Conference for Black Power, held in Newark in 1967, brought together about seven hundred delegates from all over the country. They passed this startling resolution:

> Whereas the black people in America have been systematically oppressed by their white fellow countrymen
> Whereas there is little prospect that this oppression can be terminated, peacefully or otherwise, within the foreseeable future
> Whereas the black people do not wish to be absorbed into the larger white community
> Whereas the black people in America find that their interests are in contradiction with those of white America

Whereas the black people are psychologically handicapped by virtue of their having no national homeland

Whereas the physical, moral, ethical, and esthetic standards of white American society are not those of black society and indeed do violence to the self-image of the black man

Whereas black people were among the earliest immigrants to America, having been ruthlessly separated from their fatherland, and have made a major contribution to America's development, most of this contribution having been uncompensated, and

Recognizing that efforts are already well advanced for the convening of a Constitutional Convention for the purpose of revising the Constitution of the U.S. for the first time since America's inception, then

Be it resolved that the Black Power Conference initiate a national dialogue on the desirability of partitioning the U.S. into two separate and independent nations, one to be a homeland for white and the other to be a homeland for black Americans.[15]

Professor Robert S. Browne, who read the resolution to the conference, in explaining this document, agrees that such a discussion moves in a radical direction. But he justifies it: "I have listened to the voices of my people and I know that they are desperate."[16] He likens the American situation as a bad marriage between races, for which a divorce might be the only answer. Only future events will determine this. However, we must realize that the actions of Americans *make* the future. We decide what kind of future we want.

The Meaning of the Muslims

Elijah Muhammad and his teacher W. D. Fard use and promote the biblical saying, "An eye for an eye; a tooth for a tooth." For white hatred, they offer black hatred; for white supremacy, they offer black independence; instead of Christianity—which they claim has failed the black man—they offer the Muslim religion. Perhaps the doctrines of the Temple of Islam upset white America so much because Muhammad answers white America with identical weapons—hate for hate and violence for violence.

The Muslims point out one possible way the future can move: a black society and a white society, politically, economically, and culturally independent of each other. Equality in American society is denied the black citizen; Muhammad teaches that a separate society must be formed.

And yet, recognizing the difficulties that black citizens have experienced, and the benefits Muslims have given to so many men and women, how can we approve of separatism? The United States is not a white man's country. Black men, yellow men, brown men all worked in fields, in railroads, in armies—in all areas—to build up this most powerful country. Black men lived, worked, and died here before the Irish immigration, the Italian immigration, and the hosts of Europeans who came here after 1850. African-Americans constitute part of our oldest citizenry! And yet, they are still denied their fair share of rights as citizens.

Those of us who treasure African-American contributions to our society—jazz, poetry, music, heroism, color, variety—can hardly approve of separatism. America would be much poorer without her black citizens. The answer seems to be not in separate societies of black and white, but in a different kind of struggle: personal and collective warfare against racism in America. Against every trace of pressure that would make a black citizen feel second class. America— more than any country in the world—built greatness out of variety in religion, culture, and race. Recognizing and respecting this variety is the only way to preserve this greatness, unite these states, and prevent what the Black Muslims think necessary.

footnotes

This is the official name of the movement led by the [1] Honorable Elijah Muhammad. See Elijah Muhammad, *Message to the Black Man in America* (Chicago, Muhammad's Mosque No. 2, 1965).

The standard work on the Black Muslim movement is C. [2] Eric Lincoln, *The Black Muslims in America* (Boston, Beacon Press, 1961). An important related book is by E. U. Essien-Udom, *Black Nationalism* (Chicago, University of Chicago Press, 1962).

Lincoln, *Black Muslims,* p. 10. [3]

Mr. Fard referred to himself as Mr. F. Mohammad Ali, [4] Mr. Farrad Mohammad, Professor Ford, Mr. Wali Farrad, and W. D. Fard. See Lincoln, *Black Muslims,* p. 11.

Malcolm X, *Autobiography,* p. 206 ff. [5]

Lincoln, *Black Muslims,* pp. 14–15; Essien-Udom, *Black* [6] *Nationalism,* pp. 44–45. On the back page of *Muhammad Speaks,* the official newspaper of the Nation of Islam, Mr. Muhammad is titled The Messenger of Allah. Number twelve of "What the Muslims Believe" says this: "We believe that Allah (God) appeared in the Person of Master W. Fard Muhammad, July, 1930; the long-awaited 'Messiah' of the Christians and the 'Mahdi' of the Muslims." Essien-Udom says that a dispute over the identity of W. D. Fard led to a splintering of Fard's original followers. See *Black Nationalism,* p. 44.

Lincoln, *Black Muslims,* pp. 143, 187–188. 7

Ibid., p. 29. 8

Essien-Udom, *Black Nationalism,* pp. 138–139. 9

"What the Muslims Want" #4, from *Muhammad* 10
Speaks. The Muslim Program is printed on the back page of each issue.

Malcolm X, "Letters from Mecca," in *The Black Power* 11
Revolt, Barbour, ed., p. 241.

Cleaver, *Soul on Ice,* p. 56. 12

From *Muhammad Speaks.* 13

Black Power (St. Paul, Catechetical Guild, 1968), p. 21. 14

Chronicles, Chambers, ed., pp. 281–282. 15

Ibid., p. 287. 16

13
soul food
versus steak

"Soul food"—food for the soul from the leftovers of white tables. LeRoi Jones describes it:

> All those different kinds of greens . . . once were all Sam got to eat. (Plus the pot likker, into which one slipped some throwed away meat.) Collards and turnips and kale and mustards were not fit for anybody but the woogies. . . . Did you ever hear of a black-eyed pea? (Whitey used it for forage, but some folks couldn't.) And all those weird parts of the hog? (After the pig was stripped of its choicest parts, the feet, snout, tail, intestines, stomach, etc., were all left for the "members" [i.e. slaves] who treated them mercilessly.)[1]

"Soul food" is now in fashion, even among whites. In one city, white housewives attend cooking classes in "soul food." Eldridge Cleaver, however, says something different: "The people in the ghetto want steaks. *Beef Steaks.*"[2]

This is the fact: after centuries—400 years—of working for this country, the black man in America is impatient with the leftovers, and the "crumbs from whitey's table." There is cause for complaint. Statistics taken in 1963 considered 12 percent of America's white families in the poverty belt; 42 percent of America's black families were poor. The median income for white families that year was $6,548; for non-white families it was $3,465.[3] Black unemployment is twice as high as white employment. Black people do not eat their fair share of the American pie. Unfortunately, it seems the poor are getting poorer, and the rich are getting richer. Langston Hughes put the problem in his poem "Harlem":

> Here on the edge of hell
> Stands Harlem—
> Remembering the old lies,
> The old kicks in the back,
> The old "Be patient"
> They told us before.
>
> Sure we remember.
> Now when the man at the corner store
> Says sugar's gone up another two cents,
> And bread one,
> And there's a new tax on cigarettes—
> We remember the job we never had,
> Never could get,
> And can't have now
> Because we're colored.
>
> So we stand here
> On the edge of hell
> In Harlem
> And look out on the world
> And wonder
> What we're gonna do
> In the face of what
> We remember.[4]

It is easy for people to sit around and talk about "the problem" (as long as it is the problem of someone else), or to go to church and "pray for the poor." The leaders of the black community today, however, are impatient with such platitudes. Elijah Muhammad demands even a separate territory for black people—to be supported for twenty or twenty-five years by the United States government. In his poem, Langston Hughes spoke about "what/We remember."[5] The memories are not pleasant; they do not form a glorious chapter in our history.

Pre-War Slave Castes

The Africans brought to this country to do slave labor came from very different backgrounds, nations, tribes, and even religions. In many cases they were as different as a German is from a Frenchman. Nevertheless, herded into slave ships, put on the auction block, all simply became "slaves" or "niggers." In time, however, the African slaves became American slaves, and language and religion were lost, family ties were weakened, and life was judged from the viewpoint of "Massa."[6] In place of a cultural heritage, the natural right of all people, the now American slaves fit the caste system established by the white man's economy: field hands, artisans, household workers, and freed men. For decades after the Civil War, this caste system maintained itself in various ways.

"Freed man" or "free Negro"[7] deceives us. Before or after the Civil War, the black man in America has never been free. Before the war, however, many were no longer slaves. Their "freedom" was only a half measure, however, since numerous state laws limited their actions. Despite these laws they were able by hard work and acquired trades to build up their property. By 1860, 488,000 blacks achieved this quasi-free status.[8] One estimate gives their wealth up to that time as $50,000,000. They worked at innumerable trades:

farmers, carpenters, shoemakers, bricklayers, painters, barbers, tailors, storekeepers, caterers, and so forth. After the war, this small percentage of quasi-free blacks had at least some tradition in the economic system.

We can say the same about two other castes of blacks: artisans and house workers. At least they possessed skills that would enable them to make an entrance into the competitive market after the "emancipation" that the Civil War gave them. But what about the vast majority of former slaves—the field hands? They had no education—slave owners considered this dangerous—and only one skill, farming. One answer, of course, would be to give them farms of their own. This proposal never passed. Instead, after the war, many former slaves had little choice but to work for former masters as sharecroppers.[9] There was little chance to better themselves economically. The artisans —who could have contributed much—were never permitted to enter the mainstream of American industry. The unions, which began to grow in numbers and strength only after the Civil War, prevented black workers from joining. Black workers, then, were prevented from gaining skills to help them raise themselves economically and socially. African-Americans then, because of racist union policies, have been constantly forced to the most menial positions. Herbert Hill, labor director of the NAACP, makes a searing judgment on union racism: that labor "could have been a force helping to liberate the American Negro—instead, most unions have become instruments of racial oppression." It seems strange that the unions, organized to protect working men from oppression, turned into oppressors themselves.

Liberty Without Equality

By the time of the Civil War, the North wanted liberty for the black man, but not equality. That means simply that white men did not accept black men on the same level as human beings. Take the example of the army—even President Lincoln at first opposed having blacks serve in the army.[10] After the Emancipation Proclamation was issued, the army then admitted black men to its ranks.[11] There was no equality however; they received only half the pay of a white soldier, were commanded by white officers, and organized in segregated units.[12] Despite these factors, 200,000 blacks served heroically in the Union cause, and earned twenty-two Medals of Honor.[13]

After the war and the Thirteenth, Fourteenth, and Fifteenth amendments were passed, the black man discovered he was still in slavery—the economic kind. He still served the white man, only as a sharecropper instead of slave; labor unions did not want him,[14] and even his life—given for his country—was worth only half pay. America kept the black man in two of his prewar castes: field hands and "house niggers."[15]

The Myth of Negro Business

Business makes money, and manufactures a strong middle-class economy. The Negro Business League came into existence in 1900, under the leadership of Booker T. Washington.[16] The members of this League have proposed through the years that the solution of the economic plight of the black American is business —that is, black owned and black patronized business. Despite efforts made, and despite the many words spoken on this subject, black business has failed. True, there are many such small businesses throughout the country, but they play a very small part in the over-all American economy.

What are the reasons for this failure? First of all, reasons lie with the black community itself. It has no business tradition that other ethnic groups have. Secondly, black-owned businesses are seldom patronized by whites. And third, the idea of segregated business being the black man's economic redemption is a myth. What the black minority group needs is a greater share in the huge economy of white America. In the past, opportunities to rise within the white American system were simply closed to non-whites. The money in America is held by the white majority; that is the reason why it is a myth to look at Negro business as the economic hope of the black community. In the light of this fact, we can see why so many in the Black Power movement accuse America of not sharing its wealth with its black minority group. It has not been done in the past; instead, promises are made and not kept, signs of "progress" are pointed out, and "Negro business" is encouraged.

Someone once asked Malcolm X for the names of white men who have given the most help to the black cause. Malcolm replied, in his usual sensational manner, "Hitler."[17] In explanation, he said that the demands of World War II, the many jobs left vacant by soldiers, *forced* this country to allow black people into formerly closed areas. In World War II, black people had jobs because white America needed workers. This seems part of the history of a racist society: only when forced, will concessions come. The same thing happened in the Civil War: blacks were refused by the army until the army had to accept them because of a shortage of white soldiers.

This country now enjoys the greatest prosperity the world has ever known. Television, newspapers, and magazines picture for us the wonderful products American industry turns out. Salesmen tell us these are "necessities." In today's society, people cannot be satisfied with just avoiding starvation. They want—and justly so—the fine things America has to offer. The black community realizes today that throughout its history, America's economy has been unfair to them. They are no longer willing to eat the leftovers from the white man's table, even if they call that "soul food." "They want steaks," Cleaver says.[18] There is no just reason why black Americans should not be eating as many steaks as white Americans. The answer, likewise, does not lie in charity, in the "welfare" system which dehumanizes people. The answer lies in an open economy—open to black and white.

We see the alternatives: the separate state proposed by Mr. Elijah Muhammad; the make-believe solution of Negro businesses; or the growing impatience of black Americans which becomes ever more militant. One of the first things this country did to freed men was to give them half pay as soldiers. This country still does not pay its black minority a fair wage.

Changes must come in the white-dominated economy of this country. But changes must also come from the black community. Black people have been told for decades that they are "lazy and dumb and shiftless.'"[19] Unfortunately—but understandably—too many have believed this lie. Blacks must shake off such false conceptions of themselves, bred into them by a white-dominated world. Charles Silberman, in his *Crisis in Black and White,* puts the blame on "white prejudice and Negro apathy." He says, "If all discrimination were to end immediately that alone would not materially improve the Negro's position. The unpleasant fact is that too many Negroes are unable—and unwilling—to compete in an integrated society."[20]

If black Americans have been "unable and unwilling" to compete, they have been made so by pressures within this society. Our society needs now a quiet economic revolution. The white power structure must open doors to black men; and the black minority must have the courage and self-confidence to walk through those doors. Black Americans deserve full pay from this country. They will accept no less.

Jones, "Soul Food," *Home: Social Essays* (New York, **1**
William Morrow, 1966), p. 102.

Cleaver, *Soul on Ice,* p. 29. **2**

Nathan Wright Jr., "The Crisis Which Bred Black **3**
Power," *Black Power Revolt,* Barbour, ed., p. 106.

Langston Hughes, "Harlem," *The Panther and the Lash* **4**
(New York, Knopf, 1948, 1967), p. 4.

Ibid., p. 4. **5**

See Silberman, *Crisis,* pp. 77–93. The question is asked: **6**
"What happened to transform the heroic African into
the submissive slave?" (p. 82).

Ibid., p. 93. **7**

Franklin, *Slavery to Freedom,* p. 215. **8**

Lincoln, *Negro Pilgrimage,* p. 72. **9**

Franklin, *Slavery to Freedom,* p. 273. **10**

Quarles, *Frederick Douglass,* p. 204. **11**

Franklin, *Slavery to Freedom,* p. 286. **12**

Lincoln, *Negro Pilgrimage,* p. 60. **13**

Franklin, *Slavery to Freedom,* p. 394. Herbert Hill, "La- **14**
bor Unions and the Negro," *Black Protest,* Grant, ed.,
p. 480. Logan, *Betrayal,* pp. 147–162.

Lincoln, *Sounds of the Struggle,* p. 134; Jones, *Home,* **15**
p. 73.

Franklin, *Slavery to Freedom,* p. 396. **16**

Malcolm X, *Autobiography,* p. 243. **17**

Cleaver, *Soul on Ice,* p. 29. **18**

Malcolm X, *Autobiography,* p. 29. **19**

Silberman, *Crisis*, p. 70. **20**

14
educating
white
black men

In Arkansas, Richard Wright's[1] house stood near the railroad tracks. His front yard was filled with cinders rather than grass or trees. He found the cinders useful, however, for ammunition in war games. One day his gang fought with a gang of white boys who threw broken glass instead of cinders. Richard's ear was cut, and the war ended suddenly. His troops retreated, and neighbors took him to the hospital. He brooded the rest of the afternoon about his three stitches, and the injustice of throwing glass instead of cinders:

> When night fell, my mother came from the white folks' kitchen. I raced down the street to meet her. I could just feel in my bones that she would understand. I knew she would tell me exactly what to do next time. I grabbed her hand and babbled out the whole story. She examined my wound, then slapped me.
>
> "How come yuh didn't hide?" she asked me. "How come yuh awways fightin'?"

I was outraged, and bawled. Between sobs I told her that I didn't have any trees or hedges to hide behind. There wasn't a thing I could have used as a trench. And you couldn't throw very far when you were hiding behind the brick pillars of a house. She grabbed a barrel stave, dragged me home, stripped me naked, and beat me till I had a fever of one hundred and two. She would smack my rump with the stave, and, while the skin was still smarting impart to me gems of Jim Crow wisdom. I was never to throw cinders any more. I was never to fight any more wars. I was never, never, under any conditions, to fight *white* folks again. And they were absolutely right in clouting me with the broken milk bottle. Didn't I know she was working hard every day in the hot kitchens of the white folks to make money to take care of me? When was I ever going to learn to be a good boy? She couldn't be bothered with my fights. She finished by telling me that I ought to be thankful to God as long as I lived that they didn't kill me.[2]

The Non-Education of Slaves

Throughout our country's history, white Americans have fought against the education of black Americans. In times of slavery, numerous laws forbade teaching blacks even the elements of reading and writing.[3] Of course, some exceptions existed. In New England, for example, religious motives persuaded some that all men should be able to read the Bible. Even throughout the 1700s we find evidence in New England and the north central states that some schools taught black men. In the South, the case differed. Teaching slaves —even privately—broke the law; even free blacks found difficulty in securing education. In Charleston, for example, the freeman Daniel Payne opened a school in 1829; it lasted six years, until state laws closed it.[4] Even the South, however, had exceptions. Occasionally, owners would teach some of their slaves to read and write, as in the case of Frederick Douglass: "Very soon after I went to live with Mr. and Mrs. Auld, she very kindly commenced to teach me the A, B, C. After I had learned this, she assisted me in learning to spell words of three or four letters."[5]

At this point, unfortunately, Mr. Auld discovered what his wife was doing. He forbade the continuation of the teaching, and gave his wife this bit of his philosophy:

> A nigger should know nothing but to obey his master—to do as he is told to do. Learning would *spoil* the best nigger in the world. Now, if you teach that nigger how to read, there would be no keeping him. It would forever unfit him to be a slave. He would at once become unmanageable, and of no value to his master. As to himself, it could do him no good, but a great deal of harm. It would make him discontented and unhappy.[6]

Douglass made the great discovery that—not whips or chains—but ignorance best helped the cause of slavery. Daniel Payne made this same discovery when a slaveholder said to him. "Do you know what makes the difference between master and slave? Nothing but superior knowledge."[7]

Benjamin Banneker knew the truth and the importance of this before either Douglass or Payne. Banneker, born a freeman in 1731, studied mathematics, science, and astronomy.[8] Like Benjamin Franklin, he published a series of almanacs, and he served on the presidential commission which surveyed the present city of Washington, D.C.: In correspondence with Thomas Jefferson, who owned slaves all his life,[9] Banneker objected to Jefferson's theory that blacks "are inferior to whites in the endowments both of body and mind."[10] It is ironic that before his death, Banneker was disenfranchised in the country whose capitol he had helped plan.[11]

Throughout the pre-Civil War period, however, too many whites believed Jefferson's theory; and not enough blacks were able to make the discovery that Douglass and Payne made. As a result, the great mass of blacks remained completely illiterate.

Post-War Schools

Grown men studied their alphabets in the fields, holding the "blue-back" speller with one hand while they guided the plow with the other. Mothers tramped scores of miles to towns where they could place their children in school. Pine torches illumined the dirt-floored cabins where men, women and children studied until far into the night. No mass movement has been more in the American tradition than the urge which drove Negroes toward education soon after the Civil War.[12]

Even before the end of the war, the education of former slaves began in earnest. Northern missionary alliances sent volunteers to occupied areas of the South to begin the work. One estimate states that by the last year of the war, one thousand teachers had involved themselves with the task of making slaves truly *free* by educating them. In March, 1865, one month before the war ended, Congress set up the Freeman's Bureau, to help the black man adjust to his new role in society.[13] Besides this, about one hundred privately sponsored organizations worked towards the same ends. This Bureau attempted to improve health standards, distribute needed food, resettle the homeless, and secure justice. The Freeman's Bureau, however, achieved its greatest success in education. By the end of five years, it set up—or coordinated—four thousand schools, with nine thousand teachers and a quarter of a million students. Enthusiasm ran high, even when faced with opposition and great difficulties. This work in education helped to shorten the difference between master and slave. This period also saw the founding of Negro colleges in the South like Howard, Fisk, Atlanta, and Tuskegee.[14] The latter institution achieved special importance later on because of the presence of Booker T. Washington.

Segregated Education

Segregated schools exist in the South and in the North. However, their basis differs somewhat. Segregated education in the South came about even in Reconstruction days. The schools opened by the Freeman's Bureau were segregated, since they were only for black students. The Reconstruction governments, although they began a system of public education, never succeeded in making it integrated. Eventually, the South achieved separate educational systems by the "Jim Crow" laws, which were passed largely between 1890 and 1910. The North achieved segregated education not so much through law, as through more subtle means of ghettos, districts, and "neighborhood schools." In both the North and the South segregated education has spelled inferior education for the black minority group in terms of buildings, facilities, texts, and teachers. Curriculum is another problem. In the past, the curriculum in schools has been almost exclusively geared to the needs of white students. It has neglected the black minority.

Segregated education received the approval of the courts, even the approval of the Supreme Court.[15] As early as 1849, a Boston court decided in favor of "separate but equal" schools.[16] Fifty years later, despite a Civil War, Reconstruction governments, and abolitionist fervor, the Supreme Court made this statement concerning education:

> Laws permitting, and even requiring (separation of the races) in places where they are liable to be brought into contact do not necessarily imply the inferiority of either race to the other, and have been general, if not universally, recognized as within the competency of the state legislatures in the exercise of their police power. The most common instance of this is connected with the establishment of separate schools for white and colored children, which has been held a valid exercise of the legislative power even by courts of states where the political rights of the colored race have been longest and most earnestly enforced.[17]

Racism in the South used this statement from the *Plessy* versus *Ferguson* case to justify its end of segregated education. This court decision came at a critical moment in the history of the southern states because they were, at that time, building their public school system. The Reconstruction governments passed the first laws for establishing public schools in the South. Before that, private tutors and private institutions took care of the education of the privileged. Reconstruction governments, however, moved in favor of education for everyone. But building a school system takes time, and by 1896—the *Plessy* versus *Ferguson* case—universal education in the South was still far away. Unfortunately, the decision of the Supreme Court established a precedent—segregation. From this time forward, separate education dominated the thinking, and the laws, of the South; it completely determined the still new public school system. In practice, this meant that the children of black citizens simply could not go to the same school as the children of white citizens. Even the textbooks, in some cases, differed. The principle of "separate but equal"[18] education never became a reality. Education was separate, but not equal. In some cases, for example, twenty dollars would be spent on the education of a white child, while two dollars would be spent on the education of a black child. Older black students were not permitted to attend the state universities. With such separate and unequal education, we can hardly wonder that generations of black Americans found difficulty in achieving real liberty. Remember what the slavemaster said: the difference between master and slave is superior knowledge. The lesson of history shows us that racist policies seem determined to give the black Americans inferior knowledge, and thus maintain a lower caste in society.

Ghetto Education

Northerners find it easy to criticize southern racism. In this way, perhaps, they are able to escape the fact of northern racism. This, in fact, can be more destructive than its southern counterpart. For in the South, with its separate but equal racism, a black American knew definitely that he had second-class citizenship. The North tells black Americans that they are first-class citizens, and then goes on to deny this in countless ways, including its educational system.

After 1910, many blacks chose to move into

northern areas. Where the black American moves, the white American moves out and ghettos result. Langston Hughes dramatizes the situation in his poem "Little Song on Housing."

Here I come!
Been saving all my life
To get a nice home
For me and my wife.

White folks flee—
As soon as you see
My problems
And me!

Neighborhood's clean,
But the house is old,
Prices are doubled
When I get sold:
Still I buy.

White folks fly—
Soon as you spy
My wife
And I!

Next thing you know,
Our neighbors all colored are.
The candy store's
Turned into a bar:
White folks have left
The whole neighborhood
To my black self.

White folks, flee!
Still—there is me!
White folks, fly!
Here am I![19]

The large, northern city with ghetto-segregated schools faces a huge problem. The fact is that education is separate and unequal. Educational testing shows that the performance of students in a ghetto school falls behind the scores of white children in a comfortable middle-class school. Racists would like to use these statistics for justifying their favorite doctrine of white superiority. The problem lies elsewhere, however. It lies in the very environment of a ghetto. Before school begins, a child in a ghetto situation experiences overcrowding, noise, and the lack of privacy. His imagination has little chance to grow. Besides this, even conversation with his family is difficult. So, a child from the ghetto, *before first grade,* learns less than other children. He comes to school *less prepared to learn.* Very likely reading will be more difficult, and he will fall behind in those very important first years of school. After that, catching up becomes almost impossible.

Where does the solution lie in such a huge problem? Some experts even speculate that between 50 and 80 percent of ghetto children fail to become truly educated. One view proposes integrated schools. But if neighborhoods are segregated, how can schools be integrated? One answer is bussing—taking children from one neighborhood to another school district. In some cases, this might be a fine solution. In other cases, it might do more harm than good. Taking students from a ghetto school—where they are already slow learners—and putting them in a middle-class school will only put them further behind. It might even increase their already formed sense of inferiority.

A better solution seems to be to improve the ghetto schools. Fill them with qualified and enthusiastic teachers, special curriculums, and experimental programs. One of the most needed programs seems to be the extension of preschool education, that is, begin the education of children at the age of four rather than six.

Give these small children the environment they need in order to become able to learn: color, space, toys, music, games, adults who listen and talk to them. Such nursery programs will help fight against the difficulties of ghetto living, and hopefully prepare children to take on the difficult job of education. To give such special attention to ghetto schools is only right. Society has made the ghetto, and society must then take the responsibility for this.

Conclusion

The history of this country, which declares its citizens equal, shows that the white majority constantly opposed equal education for the black minority. During the period of slavery education for blacks was illegal. After the Civil War, segregation came about in the South by law, and in the North by ghettos. In practice, segregated education has meant inferior education. In the beginning of this chapter, Richard Wright told how he had to "learn Jim Crow." If all Americans are to enjoy freedom, the future must be different than the past. This country must have no more need for master, slave, nigger, or Jim Crow. The future needs one thing—Americans who are educated to be free.

"To Richard Wright"

—Conrad Kent Rivers

You said that your people
Never knew the full spirit of
Western Civilization.
To be born unnoticed
Is to be born black,
And left out of the grand adventure.

Miseducation, denial,
Are lost in the cruelty of oppression.
And the faint cool kiss of sensuality
Lingers on our cheeks.

The quiet terror brings on silent night.
They are driving us crazy. And our father's
Religion warps his life.

To live day by day
         Is not to live at all.[20]

footnotes

Prominent American black author. Noted especially for   **1**
the publication of *Native Son,* in 1940. *Dark Symphony,*
             Emanuel and Gross, eds., pp. 222–226.
Richard Wright, "The Ethics of Living Jim Crow," in   **2**
Uncle Tom's Children (New York, Harper & Row Peren-
             nial Library, 1965), pp. 4–5.
"Teaching Negroes to Read," *Civil Rights,* Blaustein   **3**
             and Zangrando, eds., pp. 134–138.
Bergman, *Chronological History of the Negro in America*   **4**
             (New York, Bergman, 1968), p. 155.
                    Douglass, *Narrative*, p. 49.   **5**
                         Ibid., p. 49.   **6**
        Meltzer, *In Their Own Words 1619–1865,* p. 54.   **7**
Bergman, *The Chronological History of the Negro in*   **8**
             America, pp. 31–32.
        Mellon, *Early American Views,* pp. 121–122.   **9**
For Jefferson's opinions, *Early American Views,* pp.   **10**
104–108; Banneker's reply to Jefferson, Meltzer, *In Their*
Own Words, 1619–1865 (New York, Crowell, 1964), pp.
13–16; also, Franklin, *Slavery to Freedom,* pp. 156–158.

Bergman, *Chronological History of the Negro in America,* p. 32. **11**

Horace Mann Bond, quoted in E. Franklin Frazier, **12** *Black Bourgeoisie* (New York, Collier, 1962), p. 57.

Kenneth M. Stampp, *The Era of Reconstruction 1865–* **13** *1877* (New York, Vintage, 1967), pp. 131–135.

Lincoln, *Negro Pilgrimage,* pp. 66–68. **14**

Ibid., pp. 78–82. **15**

Ibid., p. 78. **16**

Civil Rights, Blaustein and Zangrando, eds., pp. 305–306. **17**

For partial texts of the *Plessy* vs. *Ferguson* case, see *Civil Rights,* Blaustein and Zangrando, eds., pp. 298–311.

Logan, *Betrayal,* pp. 105–106. **18**

Hughes, *The Panther and the Lash,* pp. 79–80. **19**

American Negro Poetry, Bontemps, ed., pp. 177–178. **20**

15
color me
black

A great American writer, Richard Wright, tells this story about a job he had as a schoolboy, and about his early ambitions to become a writer:

> The next morning I chopped wood for the cook stove, lugged in scuttles of coal for the grates, washed the front porch and swept the back porch, swept the kitchen, helped wait on the table, and washed the dishes. I was sweating. I swept the front walk and ran to the store to shop. When I returned the woman said:
>
> "Your breakfast is in the kitchen."
>
> "Thank you, ma'am."
>
> I saw a plate of thick, black molasses and a hunk of white bread on the table. Would I get no more than this? They had had eggs, bacon, coffee . . . I picked up the bread and tried to break it; it was stale and hard. Well, I would drink the molasses. I lifted the plate and brought it to my lips and saw floating on the surface of the black liquid green and white bits of mold. Goddamn . . . I can't eat this, I told

myself. The food was not even clean. The woman came into the kitchen as I was putting on my coat.

"You didn't eat," she said.

"No, ma'am," I said. "I'm not hungry."

"You'll eat at home?" she said hopefully.

"Well, I just wasn't hungry this morning, ma'am," I lied.

"You don't like molasses and bread," she said dramatically.

"Oh, yes, ma'am, I do," I defended myself quickly, not wanting her to think that I dared criticize what she had given me.

"I don't know what's happening to you niggers nowadays," she sighed, wagging her head. She looked closely at the molasses. "It's a sin to throw out molasses like that. I'll put it up for you this evening."

"Yes, ma'am," I said heartily.

Neatly she covered the plate of molasses with another plate, then felt the bread and dumped it into the garbage. She turned to me, her face lit with an idea.

"What grade are you in school?"

"Seventh, ma'am."

"Then why are you going to school?" she asked in surprise.

"Well, I want to be a writer," I mumbled, unsure of myself; I had not planned to tell her that, but she had made me feel so utterly wrong and of no account that I needed to bolster myself.

"A what?" she demanded.

"A writer," I mumbled.

"For what?"

"To write stories," I mumbled defensively.

"You'll never be a writer," she said. "Who on earth put such ideas into your nigger head?"[1]

Richard Wright Destroys the Stereotype

Despite the disapproval of his first employer—and of many people like her—Richard Wright did go on to become a writer; in fact, he became one of America's most celebrated writers. In 1940, he published his major novel, *Native Son*. This book had such an impact that one critic said, "The day *Native Son* appeared, American culture was changed forever."[2]

Why did *Native Son* cause such a sensation? The answer, simply stated, is that the book presented a realistic, a truthful picture of black Americans. And finally, a part of the American world was ready to listen. The novel did not repeat so many of the stereotypes that had been a part of the folklore of this country.

These stereotyped pictures of black Americans have hurt all Americans. Unfortunately, they have crept into every form of communication: newspapers, magazines, literature, movies, and even television. And because of this, it has molded American thinking.

The woman who hired Richard Wright to do her chores, for example, worked with the "stereotyped mind."[3] She had a certain picture of what "niggers should be."[4] And Richard Wright just didn't fit that picture at all. And, in fact, he even said he wanted to be a writer! "I don't know what's happening to you niggers nowadays,"[5] was all she could say. It was all she could say because she *didn't* know—truly—what was happening. All of us, unfortunately, work with "stereotyped

143

minds," and it's hard for us to know what's happening. Working with a "stereotyped mind" means fitting the black man into certain categories. The simplest categories are "baddie" and "goodie"—the hero and villain of melodrama. But there are more than two. One white writer made three categories into which he fit all black men: "the nigger, the 'colored person,' and the Negro—upper class."[6] Sterling Brown distinguishes seven stereotypes which have been most used in American writing: the contented slave, the wretched freeman, the comic Negro, the brute Negro, the tragic mulatto, the local color Negro, the exotic primitive.[7]

These categories have been used with such great frequency that Brown says, "The Negro has met with as great an injustice in American literature as he has in American life. The majority of books about Negroes merely stereotype Negro character."[8]

If a white American examines himself closely on the seven kinds of stereotypes listed above, he will come to the conclusion that much—however involuntary it might be—of his thinking about black men works on such stereotypes. To examine thinking, then, becomes a first step towards needed social change in our society.

The Stereotype versus the Individual

There is one action to take in order to avoid making a statement like Richard Wright's first employer made, and that action consists in taking a long, hard look at what is happening today. Much of the action in the country is taking place in the world of the black artists: the writers, dancers, painters, and musicians.

What is happening is that the black artists are taking the mask off the faces of black people. They have worn these stereotype faces long enough, as the black poet Paul Laurence Dunbar complained about in this poem:

144

We wear the mask that grins and lies,
It hides our cheeks and shades our eyes,—
This debt we pay to human guile;
With torn and bleeding hearts we smile,
And mouth with myriad subtleties.

Why should the world be overwise,
In counting all our tears and sighs?
Nay, let them only see us, while
    We wear the mask.

We smile, but, O great Christ, our cries
To Thee from tortured souls arise.
We sing, but oh, the clay is vile
Beneath our feet, and long the mile;
But let the world dream otherwise,
    We wear the mask.[9]

The poem shows in terms of the mask image, how black Americans have had to hide their true feelings, attitudes, and thoughts. The "black revolution" is a revolution of *thought,* and its leaders are the artists and thinkers of the black community. In place of the stereotype, they say here is an individual. Look at him closely. See he has faults and failures, virtues and victories. There are not three "kinds" of black men. There are not seven stereotypes. There are only individuals. Don't put a mask over them, but look at their true features. Because of such work as this by white and black authors, a new American age of honesty might be coming in the future.

Richard Wright was one black writer who would not accept the false face of the stereotype. He fought against it from that first day of work. In his life, he decided to leave the South, and later, even the United States in order to escape from it. About his early life, and his struggle against the stereotype, he says:

The white South said that it knew "niggers," and I was what the white South called a "nigger." Well, the white South had never known me—never known what I thought, what I felt. The white South said that I had a "place" in life. Well, I had never felt my "place"; or, rather, my deepest instincts had always made me reject the "place" to which the white South had assigned me.[10]

He did his work well. *Native Son* and Wright's other writings did not repeat stereotypes. This novel did not tell the white American what he wanted to hear; it told him what the black man wanted to tell him. And the news was not encouraging. One reader received it this way:

Speaking from the black wrath of retribution, Wright insisted that history can be a punishment. He told us the one thing even the most liberal white preferred not to hear: that Negroes were far from patient or forgiving, that they were scarred by fear, that they hated every minute of their suppression even when seeming most acquiescent, and that often enough they hated *us,* the decent and cultivated white men who from complicity or neglect shared in the responsibility for their plight.[11]

Behind the Mask

When we listen to blacks speaking about blacks, and not whites speaking about blacks, a different face appears from that of "the contented slave" or "the comic Negro." It comes out in Dunbar's honest poem, and in

146

Wright's refusal to fit himself into other people's categories. Most of the time that face is not a happy one. The old songs the slaves sang, for example, are not happy ones about "Ole Virginny," but ones filled with longing to get away. They express desires for heaven, for "Jordan," but not for the land they lived in as slaves.

Later on, under third-class citizenship, Jim Crow legislation, lynchings, and economic slavery in the ghetto, how could anything but a dissatisfied face be pictured? The mask did not hide a contented smile. Richard Wright has called the writings of black Americans a "tradition of bitterness":[12]

> Almost unbrokenly this tradition of lament was to roll down the decades, swelling, augmenting itself, becoming a vast reservoir of bitterness and despair and infrequent hope. This tradition of bitterness was to become so complex, was to assume such a tight, organic form, that most white people would think, upon examining it, that all Negroes had embedded in their flesh and bones some peculiar propensity toward lamenting and complaining.[13]

Besides this, there are words behind the mask which are important for white men to hear. Words in the mouth of a writer like Richard Wright say important things about the predominant white American culture in this country. They tell him who he is in relation to the black American.

LeRoi Jones, for example, makes important comments on what all of us have seen on the television, or in old movies: the picture of a few brave white men holding off the attacking hordes of non-white men. We know who the heroes will be: the whites will either drive the "natives"[14] away, or they will die as celebrated heroes. In either case, they come out with a Hollywood victory. Jones, the black writer, makes us stop and examine what a movie like this means, and what it does to our thinking:

> The three white men in the film *Gunga Din* who kill off hundreds of Indians, Greek hero-style, are part of an image of white men. The various black porters, gigglers, ghost-chumps and punkist Indians, etc., that inhabit the public image the white man has fashioned to characterize Black Men are references by Black Men to the identity of Black Men in the West, since that's what is run on them each day by white magic, i.e., television, movies, radio, etc.—the Mass Media (the *Daily News* does it with flicks and adjectives).[15]

The black writer and artist, then, can destroy stereotypes not only about the black man, but also about the white man. That is another reason why white America needs black writers and artists: to tell Americans about themselves. Not only black men hide behind the mask; white men do also. And such false faces must be destroyed before honest living and an honest society are achieved.

Richard Wright, the boy working after school, said he wanted to be a writer. Amazed, the woman he worked for asked him, "What for?"[16] Perhaps, instead of answering simply, "To write stories,"[17] he might have said that the entire country—all colors—needs the black writer to tell the truth, and to create in words a younger, more honest America.

Hopefully, in coming generations, America will provide more optimistic artistic comment than the "tradition of bitterness" that Richard Wright speaks of.

from "Dark Testament"

—Pauli Murray

Then let the dream linger on.
Let it be the test of nations,
Let it be the quest of all our days,
The fevered pounding of our blood,
The measure of our souls,—
That none shall rest in any land
And none return to dreamless sleep,
No heart be quieted, no tongue be stilled
Until the final man may stand in any place
And thrust his shoulders to the sky.
Friend and brother to every other man.[18]

footnotes

Richard Wright, *Black Boy* (New York, Harper & Row, Perennial Library, 1966), pp. 161–162. [1]

Seymour L. Gross and John Edward Hardy, *Images of the Negro in American Literature* (Chicago, University of Chicago Press, 1966), p. 18. [2]

Saunders Redding, "The Negro Writer and His Relationship to His Roots," in *Black Voices,* Chapman, ed., pp. 612–618. Especially p. 614. [3]

On the concept that black people must define themselves, in their own terms, see Stokely Carmichael and Charles V. Hamilton, *Black Power* (New York, Vintage, 1967), p. 37. [4]

Wright, *Black Boy,* p. 162. [5]

Dark Symphony, James A. Emanuel and Theodore L. Gross, eds. (New York, Free Press, 1968), p. 139. [6]

Sterling Brown, "Negro Character as Seen by White [7]

Authors," *Dark Symphony,* Emanuel and Gross, eds.,
pp. 139–171.

Ibid., p. 140. **8**

"We Wear the Mask," *The Complete Poems of Paul* **9**
Laurence Dunbar (New York, Dodd, Mead, 1940).

Wright, *Black Boy,* p. 283. See also "The Negro's Self- **10**
Image," Lincoln, *Sounds of the Struggle,* pp. 84–86.

Images of the Negro, Gross and Hardy, eds., pp. 18–19. **11**

Richard Wright, *White Man, Listen!* (New York, Anchor, **12**
1964), p. 79.

Ibid., p. 79. **13**

Jones, "The Legacy of Malcolm X, and the Coming of **14**
the Black Nation," *Home: Social Essays,* p. 247.

Ibid., p. 247. **15**

Wright, *Black Boy,* p. 162. **16**

Ibid., p. 162. **17**

American Negro Poetry, Bontemps, ed., pp. 108–109. **18**

16
don't blame
me!

The court becomes silent as the jurors enter in single file, the last man carrying the verdict all have been waiting for. With a rap of his hammer on the table, the judge orders the defendant, the United States, to stand up.

"Have you reached a verdict?" the judge asks.

"We have, your honor," the spokesman for the jury answers.

"How do you find the United States,—guilty or not guilty?"

Everyone in the room listens carefully as the words of the verdict roll out.

"We find the defendant guilty, you honor, on the following counts: kidnapping, murder, slavery, perjury, physical and mental cruelty."

"Impossible! Impossible! The verdict's impossible!"

All eyes look at the defense attorney, who jumped up as he heard the verdict.

"Will you explain yourself, sir?" the judge demands. "What do you mean, the verdict is impossible."

"It's impossible, your honor, because . . . because no one in the United States *feels* guilty."

Rage Under the Mask

Once the mask is lifted from the faces of black Americans, we see not only the "tradition of bitterness"[1] that Richard Wright spoke about, which is reflected in black literature, but also a smoldering anger. Two black psychiatrists, William Grier and Price Cobbs, have called this anger *black rage,* in their book which was recently published. Here is how they describe the origins of black rage:

> Slip for a moment into the soul of a black girl whose womanhood is blighted, not because she is ugly, but because she is black and by definition all blacks are ugly.

> Become for a moment a black citizen of Birmingham, Alabama, and try to understand his grief and dismay when innocent children are slain while they worship, for no other reason than that they are black.

> Imagine how an impoverished mother feels as she watches the light of creativity snuffed out in her children by schools which dull the mind and environs which rot the soul.

> For a moment make yourself the black father whose son went innocently to war and there was slain—for whom, for what?

> For a moment be any black person, anywhere, and you will feel the waves of hopelessness that engulfed black men and women when Martin Luther King was murdered. All black people understood the tide of anarchy that followed his death.[2]

Anger such as this—"black rage, apocalyptic and final"[3]—demands, it seems, release. Someone, somewhere, must be guilty of producing it. And yet it seems that no Americans admit any guilt in the matter. There is always someone else to blame. Men of today will blame the slaveholders of the last century, who could, in turn, blame the slave-traffickers of the century before them. The North blames the South for the slave system, while the South blames the North for ghettoes. The city blames the slum landlords, and the landlords blame the unfair urban tax system. Republicans blame Democrats, who in turn blame Republicans.

Everyone has someone to blame, and no one seems guilty

—for the death of a million Africans on their "middle passage" to this country.
—for centuries of forced labor in the "plantation system," America's own brand of the concentration camp.
—for the great waste of human potential, dignity, and happiness of millions of Americans.
—for lives which should have been enriched in this "land of the free," but were impoverished by an oppressive social system.

This system which hurt the black people of this country also hurt the white people, burdening them with a vague conviction that something, somewhere must be wrong. But no one wants to admit guilt on his own part. The great British writer, D. H. Lawrence, had this to say about American guilt:

When you are actually *in* America, America hurts, because it has a powerful disintegrative influence upon the white psyche.

It is full of grinning, unappeased demons, too, ghosts, and it persecutes the white men like some Eumenides, until the white men give up their absolute whiteness. America is tense with latent violence and resistance.[4]

Who Is Guilty?

The courtroom is in session. America has been declared guilty. This is the final decision, and all further pleas will be useless. The only way this country can stand with honesty before world opinion is *by admitting that the United States has been guilty in the past. And is still guilty in the present.* Only such an honest admission will help lift the "demons,"[5] as Lawrence calls them, from the life of this country. Otherwise, the "latent" violence he saw will only become more and more open. "Freedom for all, or slavery for all,"[6] Frederick Douglass said in the last century.

The question of personal guilt is important. The American poet, James Dickey, struggled with it in his poem "Slave Quarters":

How take on the guilt
Of slavers? How shudder like one who
made Money from buying a people[7]

The fact is, white Americans today cannot take on the "guilt/Of slavers." It seems useless to try to have guilty feelings about events that went on in the past.

But what about *black rage?* What about the courtroom charges? Is no one guilty?

The fact is that *all Americans are guilty.* All Americans in the present share blame for the unequal society that we are members of. If we cannot take on the guilt of the past, nevertheless, we can take on—and justly so—guilt for the present.

Points of Guilt

What are Americans of this generation guilty of? Perhaps in discovering this, a way to the future can be found, and also a way to diminish the "apocalyptic and final" rage.

Americans are guilty on these counts:

1. Looking at history with "white-colored glasses."
2. A failure to recognize the contributions and achievements of Americans of African descent.
3. Giving our minds to the "lie-makers" who have distorted and stereotyped men and women who are non-white.
4. Adoption of popular expressions against color: for example, "black day," "black-ball him," "black future."
5. Allowing our minds to be formed along racist lines, slogans, and attitudes.

Perhaps at the root of all this is a *failure to share the land of America*. For some reason, white men have come to think of this country as a "white man's land." It is not, and it never has been. It was a red man's land, and the black men built it up. The black population in this country goes back further in history than the millions of immigrants—Irish, Polish, Italian—who came fairly recently to this country. David Walker, as early as 1829, said this of the black man's status in this country: "America is more our country than it is the whites —we have enriched it with our *blood and tears*. The greatest riches in all America have arisen from our blood and tears."[8]

WORLD IMAGE OF U.S.
SLIPS TO 50-YEAR LOW

A congressional subcommittee report in 1968 declared that many foreigners look at this country as "a violent, lawless, overbearing, even a sick society."

One of the chief reasons for headlines such as these, was the racial situation in this country. The report had this to say:

> Foreign observers who looked upon the Americans as friendly, generous, open-minded and progressive people were profoundly shocked by the exposure of the conditions in American urban ghettos, by the massive Negro riots of the past three years and by the specter of continuing racial conflict in this country.

Racism is the sickness which infected this country at its birth, and which has made it sick throughout its history. In order to grow as a healthy society, Americans must root out the disease of racism.

One development in most recent years is the growth of black power. After looking at history, it is not difficult to see why this concept had to arise. History shows us that the whites have never dealt fairly with the blacks. This is unfortunate, but the evidence of history shows this clearly. Because of this growing awareness of the facts, *black men today simply don't trust white men.* Martin Luther King was, perhaps, the last of the great black leaders who put his faith in the goodwill of the white community. He was assassinated[9] for his faith and goodwill.

The burden today is not on the blacks to "prove themselves." Rather, it is on the white men of the country to prove themselves—that they can live without white power, in peace and harmony with people of different colored skins. No white man should need a "nigger" as a scapegoat.

We inherited the past. The future is ours. The country has within it the possibility of evolving into a *world-community* to make other countries look with envy upon our spiritual wealth, rather than our material wealth. At the same time, the seeds of racism threaten it with internal revolt, world-wide disapproval, and a road leading downward.

Perhaps—only perhaps—if white Americans recognize their guilt, and work fast enough to change things, black Americans might join in building up a new society, which must be different from the past. The guilt is white. The future, hopefully, will be technicolor.

from **"Dark Symphony"**

—Melvin B. Tolson

Black slaves singing *One More River to Cross*
In the torture tombs of slave ships,
Black slaves singing *Steal Away to Jesus*
In jungle swamps,
Black slaves singing *The Crucifixion*
In slave pens at midnight,
Black slaves singing *Swing Low, Sweet Chariot*
In cabins of death,
Black slaves singing *Go Down, Moses*
In the canebrakes of the Southern Pharaohs.

They tell us to forget
The Golgotha we tread . . .
We who are scourged with hate,
A price upon our head.
They who have shackled us

Require of us a song,
They who have wasted us
Bid us o'erlook the wrong.

They tell us to forget
Democracy is spurned.
They tell us to forget
The Bill of Rights is burned.
Three hundred years we slaved,
We slave and suffer yet:
Though flesh and bone rebel,
They tell us to forget!

Oh, how can we forget
Our human rights denied?
Oh, how can we forget
Our manhood crucified?
When Justice is profaned
And plea with curse is met,
When Freedom's gates are barred,
Oh, how can we forget?[10]

footnotes

Wright, *White Man, Listen!,* p. 79. **1**

Grier and Cobbs, *Black Rage,* pp. 176–177. **2**

Ibid., p. 177. **3**

D. H. Lawrence, *Studies in Classic American Literature* **4**
(New York, Viking, 1964), p. 51.

Ibid., p. 51. **5**

Quarles, *Frederick Douglass,* p. 187. **6**

James Dickey, *Poems 1957–1967* (New York, Macmillan, **7**
Collier Books, 1968), p. 237.

Franklin, *Slavery to Freedom,* p. 240. **8**

I Have a Dream (New York, Life-Time Books, 1968). **9**

Tolson, *Rendezvous with America* (New York, Dodd, **10**
Mead, 1944).

Acknowledgments

All photographs in this book were taken by Harrison Branch.

We wish to thank the following for permission to use the excerpts appearing in this book.

Black Rage by William H. Grier and Price M. Cobbs, Basic Books, Inc., Publishers, New York, 1968.

"If We Must Die" by Claude McKay from *Selected Poems of Claude McKay*. Copyright 1953 by Bookman Associates, Inc. Used by permission of Twayne Publishers, Inc.

"Outcast" by Claude McKay from *Selected Poems of Claude McKay*. Copyright 1953 by Bookman Associates, Inc. Used by permission of Twayne Publishers, Inc.

"Booker T. and W.E.B." by Dudley Randall. Reprinted by permission of Broadside Press.

"We Wear the Mask." Reprinted by permission of Dodd, Mead & Company, Inc., from *The Complete Poems of Paul Laurence Dunbar.*

"Dark Symphony." Reprinted by permission of Dodd, Mead & Company, Inc., from *Rendezvous with America* by Melvin B. Tolson.

The Autobiography of Malcolm X with the assistance of Alex Haley. Reprinted by permission of Grove Press, Inc. Copyright © 1964 by Alex Haley and Malcolm X. Copyright © 1965 by Alex Haley and Betty Shabazz.

"The Ethics of Living Jim Crow." From pp. 4–5, *Uncle Tom's Children* (Perennial Classic Edition) by Richard Wright. Copyright 1937 by Richard Wright. Reprinted by permission of Harper & Row, Publishers, Inc.

From pp. 161–162, *Black Boy* (Perennial Classic Edition) by Richard Wright. Copyright 1937, 1942, 1944, 1945, by Richard Wright. Reprinted by permission of Harper & Row, Publishers, Inc.

From Slavery to Freedom by John Hope Franklin. Copyright 1947, 1956, 1967 by Alfred A. Knopf, Inc. Reprinted by permission of the publisher.

"Harlem." Copyright 1948 by Alfred A. Knopf, Inc. Reprinted

B3164